D&L Trail, Towns & Cul[...]

THE
STONE COAL WAY

A Guide to Navigating
Delaware & Lehigh National Heritage Corridor
through Eastern Pennsylvania

Written by: Tom Shealey
Edited by: Elissa G. Marsden

Published by: Delaware & Lehigh National Heritage Corridor
C. Allen Sachse, Executive Director

Partially funded by:
United States Department of the Interior
Pennsylvania Department of Conservation & Natural Resource

Special thanks to Lance Metz and the staff of the National Canal Museum, Easton, PA

Design by: Workhorse Design, Lehighton, PA
Printed by: Chernay Printing, Coopersburg, PA

www.delawareandlehigh.org

Table of Contents

INTRODUCTION

The Stone That Burns

To appreciate the D&L Trail and Corridor, you need to understand what's underfoot and the impact coal had on the land and people

To say the D&L Trail and Corridor are linked to coal is akin to saying a chicken has something to do with an egg.

It's a tale every youngster hears in history class. Some unsuspecting soul strolls through an untouched plot of land, looks down and discovers: A) gold; B) silver; C) oil; D) some other valuable product born under the earth's surface. Riches follow, as do commerce and development, and the land is forever changed.

Philip Ginder discovering "stone coal" at Summit Hill.

A similar scenario unfolded in 1791 in what is now Summit Hill in Carbon County. A miller named Philip Ginder was searching for a new millstone when he found a black, shiny rock. Having heard

of "stone coal," he took the chunk to a blacksmith and lo and behold, it burned.

By simply bending down to inspect an odd stone at his feet, Ginder helped launch what would become Pennsylvania's powerful anthracite mining industry. His accidental discovery would ripple through two and a half centuries, affect countless generations of families in both the United States and abroad, give rise to the American Industrial Revolution, and even play a part in the winning of two world wars.

Coal is the reason the D&L Trail exists. Coal is the reason many area towns sprouted. It's the reason America's iron and steel industries became an international force. And the reason the Lehigh and Delaware Canals made such a huge impact on this region's development. You get the idea.

The type of coal found here is anthracite, also known as "stone coal" because of its rock-like hardness. Bituminous is the soft, easy-to-burn type. Anthracite is created over millions of years as countless layers of sediment compress plant debris from swamps until it becomes hard. As the landscape heaved and buckled over the eons, creating the Appalachian and Pocono Mountains in the process, anthracite appeared atop hills and waited under valleys in seams or veins 2 to 12 feet thick.

Because of anthracite's historical importance and its rich and distinctive impact on both cultural and natural resources, in 1988 Congress designated the Delaware & Lehigh National Heritage Corridor. Its backbone is the D&L Trail, a 165-mile path stretching from the coal-rich, forested mountains of Wilkes-Barre to Bristol near the Atlantic Ocean. The D&L Trail follows the route stone coal took from mine to market, winding through northern mountains and along the banks of the Lehigh and Delaware Rivers.

Trail & Corridor

The D&L Trail is a gravel path that exposes you to some of Pennsylvania's finest wild lands, waterfalls, wildflowers and wildlife. Yet it's also a concept, a passage through time that carries you back to an era when ingenuity, unflagging determination and an unbreakable entrepreneurial spirit created a workingman's Promised Land. This extraordinary success story, along with the region's natural, cultural and recreational resources, combine to produce a remarkable trail experience like no other; one that carries you through three distinct "worlds" where the character of the land and its people were shaped by coal. The Corridor *is* this unique blend of trail, town and culture along the stone coal way.

Barred Owl is one of many birds of prey found along the D&L Trail.

Hike or bike the D&L Trail and you'll encounter:
- Free-flowing rivers that are a paddler's dream; steep gorges with some of the best rock climbing and hiking around; and lush woodlands still as wild and

Canal and river flow side-by-side through the Lehigh Valley.

untouched as they were when pioneers first arrived.

• Traces of coal mining's dramatic impact on the land and its people.

• The remains of an extraordinary 19th century coal-transport network consisting of gravity railroads, "bear trap" locks, and hand-dug canals. (Read on to learn about these and other D&L Trail-related innovations that transformed American business and industry.)

• Sites where ideas surfaced that later became the foundation of the American Constitution; the concepts of religious freedom, separation of church and state, mutual responsibility between government and the people, and equality among men were all born here.

• Farms, villages and towns—some dating back to the 1700s—that have stood the test of time, and are a key ingredient in the trail's appeal.

< *Please open to Delaware & Lehigh National Heritage Corridor Map*

Four generations lived at the Germanic Troxell-Steckel Farmstead in Egypt.

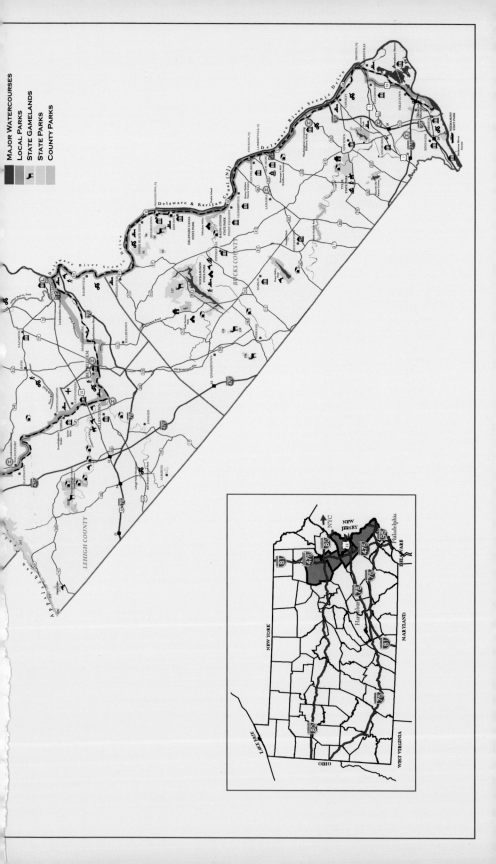

MAJOR WATERCOURSES
LOCAL PARKS
STATE GAMELANDS
STATE PARKS
COUNTY PARKS

Delaware & Lehigh National Heritage Corridor

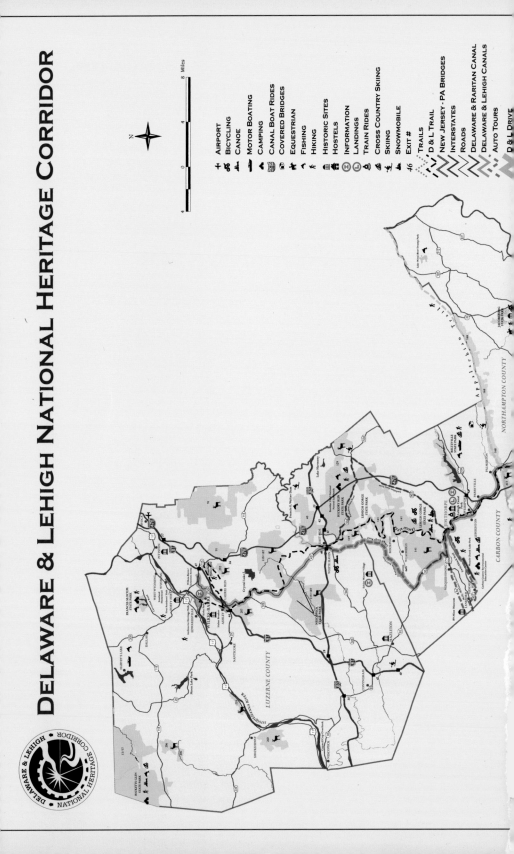

N

4   0   4   8 Miles

✈ Airport
♨ Bicycling
Canoe
Motor Boating
Camping
Canal Boat Rides
Covered Bridges
Equestrian
Fishing
Hiking
Historic Sites
Hostels
Information
Landings
Train Rides
Cross Country Skiing
Skiing
Snowmobile
46 Exit #

Trails
D & L Trail
New Jersey - PA Bridges
Interstates
Roads
Delaware & Raritan Canal
Delaware & Lehigh Canals
Auto Tours
D & L Drive

One trail… three worlds… and a hard, black tie that binds it all together. It's an amazing journey—a story just waiting to be revealed, so turn the pages and you'll be on your way. Like Philip Ginder, you'll be surprised at the discoveries that lie before you.

For More Information Contact:
Delaware & Lehigh National Heritage Corridor
A Pennsylvania State Heritage Park
1 South Third Street – 8th Floor
Easton, PA 18042
610-923-3548
www.delawareandlehigh.org

Background
From coal and canal, a culture and a pathway arise

Remnants of canals and railroads can be found all along the D&L Trail. This tunnel was a part of the Buck Mountain Gravity Railroad at Rockport.

miles west of Mauch Chunk (now known as Jim Thorpe). As the industry grew, mine shafts (some 2,000 feet long) bore down into the earth and the work became more labor intensive and dangerous.

Early attempts to sell anthracite in cities were not too successful because homeowners and housewives liked using wood. The more modern-thinking people who did use coal preferred soft bituminous because unlike anthracite, it required no forced-air draft to burn efficiently. Attitudes changed during the War of 1812 when English warships blockaded major American ports, and shut off soft coal supplies coming out of Virginia and England. To help convince people to

Two Philadelphia businessmen, Josiah White and Erskine Hazard, were among the first to see anthracite's potential to replace logs and charcoal as home heating and industrial fuels. The first excavations, hacked out of hillsides by local German farmers and English settlers, were surface mines at Summit Hill nine

Captain Irv Grant Emory on the Delaware Canal.

burn anthracite, White and Hazard gave some housewives cookstoves with draft and venting capabilities. By 1830 the market for their coal was healthy. As forests became decimated through uncontrolled clear cutting, more and more people converted to clean, hot burning anthracite. Iron furnaces along the Lehigh River shifted to anthracite by the 1840s. The more-efficient-burning coal propelled the growth of regional industry.

In the early to mid-1800s, a lengthy network of locks, canals and towpaths was built to ship anthracite, further aiding the mining industry's growth. Then in 1862, a massive flood destroyed all the dams, locks, canal boats and villages along the Upper Grand Division of the Lehigh Canal (between White Haven and Jim Thorpe). Thus a new era began, as coal shipping shifted to railroads. Asa Packer's Lehigh Valley Railroad, which ran from Mauch Chunk to Easton and on

BREAKERS: Where coal was processed into clean, uniform sizes for sale. The task was handled by "breaker boys," typically 8-15 years old, and old men too weak to handle more strenuous mine work. They sat and hand-picked slate and other impurities from the coal, and the refuse was dumped into what were known as culm piles. At least 800 breakers were built near various mine shafts, with one of largest in Ashley (south of Wilkes-Barre off I-81, where its remains are still visible today).

SUCCESS AND PROSPERITY: Of all the towpath canal systems in the U.S., the Delaware and Lehigh Canals operated the longest and were the last to shut down (1942).

95 TONS: Weight of the average coal boat heading down the Lehigh Navigation. Because shallow spots in the slackwater pools impeded weighty boats, canals were dug, dams were built, and "bear trap" locks were devised to hold water in each canal when closed. The resulting Lehigh Navigation System was constructed by mostly Irish immigrants escaping famine at home. Work started in 1827 and coal was shipped downriver from Mauch Chunk to Easton by 1829.

"NIGHT HAWKER": A type of lantern hung in the bow of canal boats at night.

FIST FIGHTS: Common at locks when boatmen tried to pass others already in line.

to New York City, was the first rail line to have a significant impact. The Lehigh & Susquehanna Railroad, Reading Railroad and the Pennsylvania Railroad also moved into the area, creating competition for shipping coal and other goods. Investment by J.P. Morgan, Cornelius Vanderbilt and other entrepreneurs gave railroads leverage to squeeze coal mining operators and the immigrants they employed.

As a result, labor troubles became a regular occurrence for both coal mining and railroad operations. There was also a stoppage by boatmen on the Lehigh Canal. Dangerous work conditions, disagreements among ethnic groups in the mines, competition between coal marketers and carriers, as well as low pay led to strikes every few years. Sabotage, arson and killings became common, and gave rise to labor unions, the most

powerful becoming the United Mine Workers.

Coal's prominence continued to slide in World War I as oil gained popularity as a home heating fuel. This was due to the fact that it was more efficient, economical and cleaner burning. As well, bootleggers sold anthracite for bargain rates and undercut the coal industry's prices.

A severe blow to Pennsylvania's deep mines was the Knox Mine Disaster on Jan. 22, 1959, when miners accidentally drilled through to the Susquehanna River. Twelve men drowned and the entire Wyoming Valley system of mines flooded.

While only a few strip mines operate today, the remaining towpaths and rail-trails provide the foundation of the D&L Trail.

Trail users will find a placid path today, very different from the perilous conditions once found here.

The D&L Trail includes:
- An abandoned railroad route that will become a trail, running from Ashley, near Wilkes-Barre, to White Haven.
- Canals that ran from White Haven to Bristol, some still in good shape, others destroyed by time and floods. The towpath alongside the canals, where boat-towing mules once trod, is today's trail.
- The still "watered" Delaware Canal running from Easton to Bristol; Except for a few spots, you can paddle the canal's waters to Morrisville.
- Rural, urban and suburban lands, mountains and sea coast, more than 100 historic villages and farms, natural beauty and cultural sites, and both active and passive recreational opportunities.

The trail passes through three distinctive "worlds":

Waterfalls, like this one in Lehigh Gorge State Park, are numerous.

- Carbon and Luzerne Counties (west of the Pocono Plateau), where anthracite coal was mined. Along the northern trail, much of the landscape is still natural and has a wilderness feel. Small towns remain amidst the forests, hills, savannas and river valleys.
- Lehigh and Northampton Counties, home to the iron and steel industries that prospered from the discovery of coal. The Trail's mid-section is characterized by hills and a fertile river valley, with easy-to-reach communities shaped by industry and commerce that still embrace the natural environmental qualities of the river and canals.

Barn at Tinicum Park, Bucks County.

• Bucks County, through which coal-laden boats passed on the way to Philadelphia and other markets. The southern third of the trail through the Delaware River Valley offers a more expansive landscape, where a free-flowing river and harnessed canal waters shaped the bucolic countryside, vibrant small towns and modern suburbs you see today. It's no wonder this blend of new and old is beloved by artists, past and present.

You'll also find along the trail:
• 9 National Historic Landmarks
• 6 National Recreation Trails
• 2 National Natural Landmarks
• 100s of sites listed in the National Register of Historic Places
• 7 State Parks
• 3 State Historical Sites
• 2 state scenic rivers
• 1 National Scenic River
• 14 State Game Lands

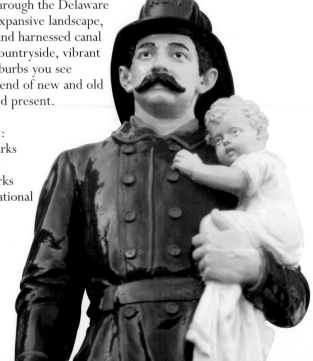

One Canal System, Two Vastly Different Effects on the Land

Though the Lehigh and Delaware Canals merged to create part of a grand transportation system stretching from the Appalachians to the Atlantic, the waterways had vastly different effects on their surrounding lands.

The Lehigh Canal system generated a great deal of industrial development in the form of mining and the accompanying infrastructure. It gave rise to many towns and offshoot businesses: timber cutting and sawmills; steel and silk mills; and one of the largest tanneries in the U.S., to name only a few businesses that once thrived here.

The Delaware Canal, on the other hand, was a means of shipping goods and establishing commerce—an economic and physical link. There was little if any industrial impact on the rural, farm region it flowed through. Farmers

had overland routes for their dairy products, grains, fruits and vegetables, only occasionally using the Canal. They did not solely depend on it for their transport needs, as did businesses to the north. As a result, most of Bucks County avoided the industrial boom seen in the counties upriver. However, the land became more valuable in the 1900s for residential use.

Lehigh Gorge and Delaware Canal State Parks offer the most continuous stretches of trail along the D&L.

Say "trail" and four out of five people will think of a well-worn earthen ribbon that carries you into the woods, far from all things urban. The D&L Trail does just that, but it also travels through communities and towns that lend character and personality to this multi-faceted route. These urban outposts speak volumes about our history.

Market towns were crossroads commercial centers, providing a variety of goods and services to a regional community. Some housing and commercial ventures in these towns predate the Canal. Examples: White Haven and Jim Thorpe.

Jim Thorpe, formerly Mauch Chunk, was a center for commerce and transportation.

Lumber towns, situated along waterways so harvested logs could easily float downstream, served as points where

Log rafts were used to get lumber to local mills.

goods passed through en route to other destinations. Saw, shingle and woodworking mills often cropped up here. Examples: Lehigh Tannery, and Lumberville.

Canal towns primarily served shippers of goods, especially anthracite coal. These towns were often located near locks, coal yards and boat yards, where Canal users patronized stores, inns and taverns. Examples: Weissport, Walnutport, Freemansburg, New Hope and Bristol.

Anthracite towns were the coal towns. Here you might find nearby mines, towering breakers where coal was cleaned and sorted, company-owned housing and church spires reflecting immigrant workers' diverse ethnicity. Examples: Lansford, Eckley and Summit Hill.

Industrial towns were, quite simply, where industries (steel, iron, slate, and cement) were born during the American Industrial Revolution as a result of the Lehigh & Delaware Canals. Examples: Slatington, Bethlehem, Allentown, Northampton, Easton and Catasauqua.

What's a Heritage Corridor?

While not as well known as national parks or monuments, a National Heritage Corridor (NHC) is just as noteworthy—if not more so.

In federal legalese, NHC status recognizes an area that's historically, culturally, environmentally and/or visually significant, and therefore warrants federal action designed to protect and promote the land. On Nov 18, 1988, President Ronald

Reagan signed the order creating the Delaware & Lehigh National Heritage Corridor. The canals, rivers, towpaths, old railroad right-of-ways, as well as the natural, cultural and recreational resources that comprise the D&L Trail, *plus* a buffer zone on either side of the trail, make up this Corridor. The D&L offers limitless opportunities to explore, discover and relive history. The National Park Service serves as a partner, facilitator, and advisor—it does not acquire or manage heritage areas or regulate private property. Think of the D&L Corridor as a "living national park," owned by many parties, and managed through voluntary partnerships. The D&L was also designated a State Heritage Park by the PA Department of Conservation & Natural Resources.

Timeline—A Brief History

1791- Philip Ginder discovers "stone coal" anthracite near Summit Hill.

1815- Seeking efficient-burning fuel, Quaker wire-mill owner Josiah White and partner Erskine Hazard discover circulating air makes the hard coal burn.

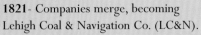

1817- White and Hazard lease coal lands, form Lehigh Coal Co.

1820- To ship coal on Lehigh River, they launch Lehigh Navigation Co. and make river navigable by constructing locks and dams from Mauch Chunk (now Jim Thorpe) to Easton. Initially, arks traveled one way.

1821- Companies merge, becoming Lehigh Coal & Navigation Co. (LC&N).

1825- As anthracite gains favor as a fuel, shipments skyrocket: 28,393 tons moved from mountains to market along Lehigh River.

1827- Commonwealth officials OK construction of 60-mile-long Delaware Division of the Pennsylvania Canal, from Easton to Bristol. Farmers and Irish immigrants hand-dig canal along old stagecoach and Lenni-Lenape routes.

White agrees to link with new Delaware Canal; starts building canals from Mauch Chunk to Easton, so shipping isn't dependent on unpredictable Lehigh River.

1829- The 46-mile Lehigh Canal opens; empty boats can return upstream to be reloaded, instead of being dismantled downstream.

1831 to 1833- Delaware Canal opens and connects with Lehigh Canal at Easton, creating continuous link between Mauch Chunk and Bristol on Atlantic Coast.

1834- At Easton, Lehigh Canal joins with New Jersey's Morris Canal, providing access to New York Harbor.

1837- State approves building railroad connecting Lehigh Canal with North Branch Canal on the Susquehanna River; result is Lehigh & Susquehanna Railroad (L&SRR) between White Haven and Wilkes-Barre.

1838- To reach northern Wyoming Valley coal fields, LC&N extends canal 26 miles from Mauch Chunk to White Haven.

1846- A 165-mile-long, rail-and-water shipping network is in place from Wyoming Valley near Wilkes-Barre to Bristol on Delaware River tidewater.

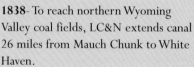

1855- Entrepreneur Asa Packer finances Lehigh Valley Railroad (LVRR) between Mauch Chunk and Easton; tracks later extended to Wilkes-Barre and eventually New York Harbor and Buffalo.

1862- Flood destroys structures between White Haven and Mauch Chunk. Instead of rebuilding, LVRR races to build north from Mauch Chunk to White Haven, increasing rail popularity and diminishing canal's importance.

1868- Railroads thrive; L&SRR extended from White Haven to Mauch Chunk, creating continuous rail line between Mauch Chunk and Wilkes-Barre.

1871- Central Railroad of New Jersey (CNJ) leases L&SRR and enters anthracite shipping business.

1917- LC&N peaks during World War I, producing 4 million tons a year and employing 9,000 people.

1931- In midst of Great Depression, 50 miles of Delaware Canal (Raubsville to Bristol) are deeded to Commonwealth; canal becomes recreation and heritage resource, and re-named Theodore Roosevelt State Park to honor former president and preservationist.

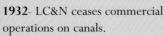

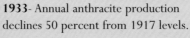

1932- LC&N ceases commercial operations on canals.

1933- Annual anthracite production declines 50 percent from 1917 levels.

1940- Ten-mile section from Easton to Raubsville added to Delaware Canal Park.

1954- Declining market forces LC&N to close Panther Valley's deep mines.

1962- Cash-strapped LC&N starts to sell canal holdings. Easton pays $45,000 for 7.5-mile section through town and names it for Hugh Moore, founder of Dixie Cup Co. who aids purchase.

1965- Former CNJ right-of-way becomes Lehigh Gorge Rail-Trail, and eventually the D&L Trail.

1974, '78- Delaware Canal listed on National Register of Historic Places, and declared a National Historic Landmark.

1989- By popular demand, name changed from Theodore Roosevelt State Park to Delaware Canal State Park.

1990- Delaware Canal towpath designated a National Heritage Trail.

2000- The D& L Trail (both Lehigh and Delaware towpaths) receives Millennium Trail designation by White House Millennium Council.

Today- Delaware and Lehigh canals represent most intact canal/towpath system in U.S.

WILKES-BARRE TO JIM THORPE

Outdoor Adventure and Recreation in the Land of Anthracite

The landscape of the Wyoming Valley Levee System.

In mining terms, the D&L Trail begins in an anthracite Mother Lode: the Wyoming Valley in Luzerne County, home to major hard-coal supplies and where the mine-to-market process started. The legacy of this land is one of intense mining, industrial development and a rich mix of ethnic cultures. While Ice Age glacier travel (12,000 years ago) did leave prehistoric scarring of hillsides, plus the occasional boulder field created by glacial outwash, the Wyoming Valley's dramatic landscape also bears the proud scars of its anthracite-mining heritage.

Besides its geological, historical and industrial significance, this is a striking landscape rich in natural resources and outdoor recreation opportunities that set it apart from the rest of the D&L Trail's route.

The 17-mile Wyoming Valley is linear, with Campbell's Ledge and the city of Pittston to the north and Tillbury's Knob and Nanticoke to the south. Wilkes-Barre, the county seat, is at the Valley's center while the mighty Susquehanna River flows through. Green, wooded hillsides slide smoothly into the valley floor, where anthracite deposits were eventually discovered, triggering the urban development that resulted in a string of towns, industries, mines, roads and rail lines to the south.

Today, the Wyoming Valley's forested ridges and unique natural areas sharply contrast with former industrial and mining communities that maintain rich architectural and cultural ties to the past. The region's pioneering spirit can still be felt here.

Wilkes-Barre
Historically and economically, where the D&L Trail story begins

An early 20th century miner's family dressed for a wedding.

Glance at the accompanying maps and you'll probably assume Wilkes-Barre is the northerly starting point—or trailhead—for the D&L Trail. Your assumption would be correct. Almost.

In Colonial times, New England "Yankees" settled in the Wyoming Valley. Then in the late 1800s, hundreds of thousands of immigrants flocked to the region to work the mines. The accompanying growth they triggered, coupled with inevitable economic and cultural changes, transformed the rural farming region into a thriving urban center.

Because Wilkes-Barre was located at the heart of the anthracite fields, and thus smack in the middle of development, it became the region's financial center and home to rich and powerful entrepreneurs whose business ventures affected the railroad-and-canal system that stretched 165 miles southward to Bristol.

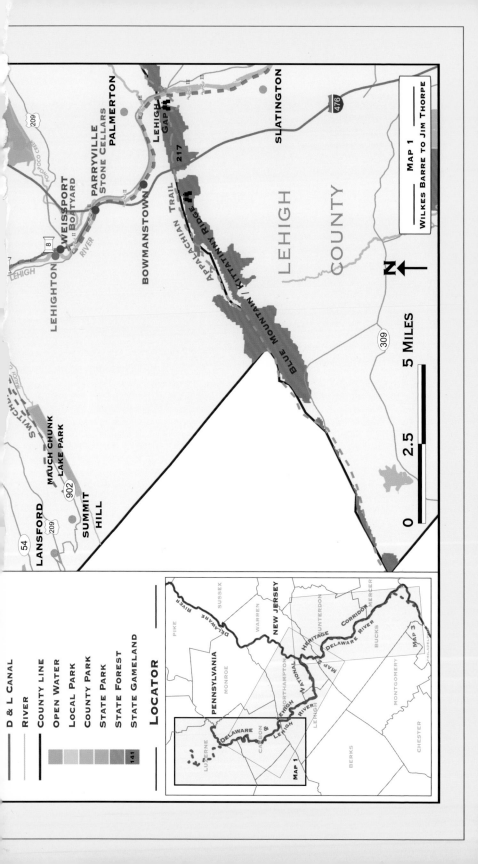

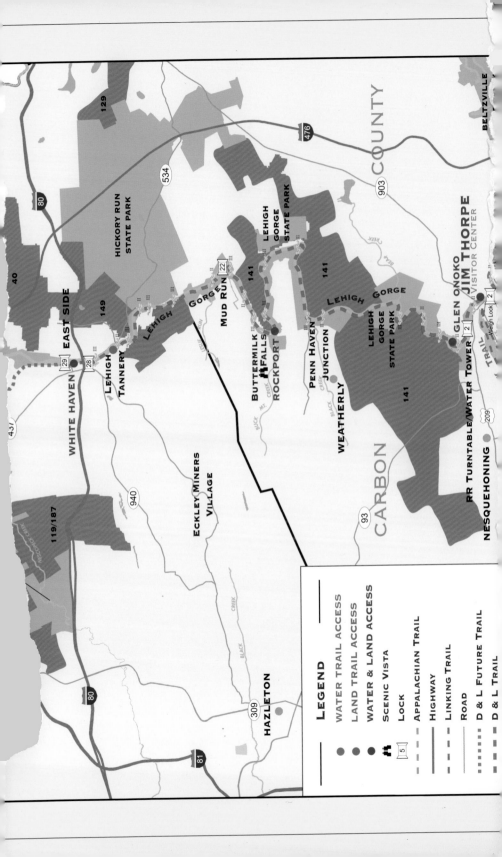

LEGEND

WATER TRAIL ACCESS
LAND TRAIL ACCESS
WATER & LAND ACCESS
SCENIC VISTA
LOCK
APPALACHIAN TRAIL
HIGHWAY
LINKING TRAIL
ROAD
D & L FUTURE TRAIL
D & L TRAIL

HICKORY RUN STATE PARK

LEHIGH GORGE STATE PARK

LEHIGH GORGE

LEHIGH GORGE STATE PARK

EAST SIDE

WHITE HAVEN

LEHIGH TANNERY

MUD RUN

BUTTERMILK FALLS

ROCKPORT

PENN HAVEN JUNCTION

WEATHERLY

ECKLEY MINERS VILLAGE

HAZLETON

CARBON COUNTY

GLEN ONOKO

JIM THORPE
VISITOR CENTER

RR TURNTABLE/WATER TOWER

NESQUEHONING

BELTZVILLE

Weigh Lock

129

534

476

903

40

149

22

141

141

141

80

940

431

119/187

309

81

93

209

28

29

5

2

So it's safe to say the D&L Trail is historically, philosophically, economically and even emotionally connected with Wilkes-Barre. It's just not yet physically linked to the city because design issues need to be resolved. Until land-use matters are settled, you'll have to head a few miles south to White Haven to start your journey at the current northern D&L trailhead.

Meanwhile, in Wilkes-Barre you can walk the paths and levee trails that pass through Kirby Park, or take a Walking Tour of the River Street National Historic District, which includes stately mansions and well-preserved structures from bygone times. This was once home to the thriving Wilkes-Barre Lace Manufacturing Co., as well as major financial, manufacturing and mercantile concerns that were supported by canals and railroads. In 1849, mill worker Richard Jones founded the Vulcan Iron Works, which eventually employed 1,600 men and

Coming Soon:
The Real Northern Trailhead

Once design issues are resolved—hopefully in a year or two—the D&L Trail's northern starting point will take its rightful place near Wilkes-Barre.

The plan calls for the trail to proceed north from its current trailhead in White Haven, passing the village of Mountaintop along the former Lehigh Valley Railroad (LVRR) line. The path will link to the Seven Tubs Natural Area, and follow the abandoned LVRR right-of-way to Wilkes-Barre Mountain. Eventually, the D&L Trail will stop at the site of a proposed Luzerne County Visitor's Center south of I-81. The center will be the official northern trailhead.

< Please open to Delaware & Lehigh National Heritage Corridor
Map 1—Wilkes-Barre to Jim Thorpe

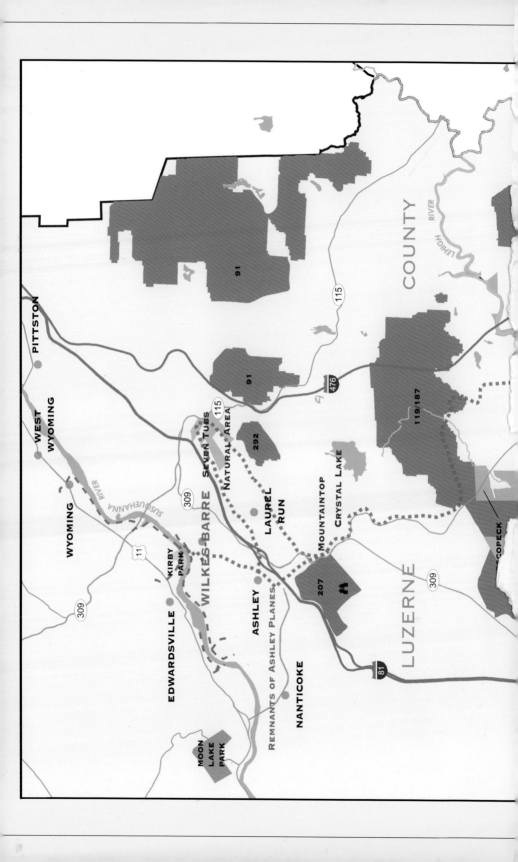

The Moorish Revival-style Irem Temple is a prominent architectural landmark in Wilkes-Barre.

produced some of the most dependable and sought-after locomotives and mine equipment of the day. In 1857 a city-based brewery opened. It produced 200,000 barrels of beer annually by the turn of the century. Silk and garment mills became major employers for miners' wives, and of course, the mines continued to dominate the economic landscape.

The first documented burning of anthracite occurred in Wilkes Barre. In 1808 Judge Jesse Fell found that circulating air made the hard-to-burn coal an efficient heat source. This discovery helped change Luzerne County from quiet frontier to a thriving region where mining was king.

One of the best places to quickly glimpse Wilkes-Barre's past is the Luzerne County Historical Society Museum on Franklin Street. It has Native American exhibits, anthracite coal displays and presentations that highlight important natural and cultural events of the Wyoming Valley. Wilkes-Barre Commons, the Kirby Theater, Irem Temple, and the mighty Susquehanna River are also nearby, as is the Luzerne County Courthouse, one of Pennsylvania's most impressive architectural masterpieces.

The 1769 Dennison House in nearby Forty Fort was home to one of the original 40 families to first settle the Wyoming Valley. The colonial-era landmark was modeled after the family's ancestral home in Connecticut. Special events at the Homestead include an encampment of the 24th Connecticut Regiment, and the reenactment of the 1778 Battle of Wyoming. It is listed on the National Register of Historic Places.

The Levee Trail

Destructive floods beget a calm, healthful hiking experience.

Since 1784 the Susquehanna River has overflowed its banks 79 times, causing loss of life and property, and resulting in billions of dollars in damages. To keep the mighty river—affectionately known as the "sleeping giant"— from doing future harm, a series of levees were constructed. So far the earthen banks have kept flood waters away from Wilkes-Barre and other Wyoming Valley towns.

Hikes to try: The levees have also yielded a trail system affiliated with the D&L Trail. The Wyoming Valley Levee System Trail is a popular 15-mile, paved path on top of the dikes at river's edge. The loop trail consists of four theme-related levees:

1. ***First Resident's Path,*** on the west bank, extends through parts of Wyoming and Forty Fort. Wayside signs tell tales of the early pioneer days, including conflicts between Native Americans and the settlers.
2. ***Anthracite Heritage Walk*** winds through Kingston and Edwardsville, and focuses on the coal industry.
3. ***Plymouth Passage*** highlights the diverse cultures and industries that shaped the community.
4. ***Riverside Ramble,*** on the east bank, has signs offering stories about the architecture, businesses, arts and agriculture in Wilkes-Barre and Hanover.

The Levee Trail will join with other paths, including the D&L Trail, to create

routes that can take days to complete, or a single afternoon. It all depends on your endurance, time and desires.

The centrally located, multi-use Levee Trail is suitable for all types of family activities, and is part of the Wyoming Valley Wellness Trails Initiative, with its goal of improving community health and quality of life by increasing opportunities for an active lifestyle.

Seven Tubs Natural Area

Winter or summer, Seven Tubs cascades downward into icy pools.

The highlight of this 600-acre Luzerne County Park is a series of holes or depressions etched in the bedrock by glacial meltwater. These "tubs" are perpetually filled by a series of cascading ponds, and are located just off PA 115. Be aware: the water is icy cold even in July, and the park closes during winter months.

Ashley

Where boys broke coal and became men

If Wilkes-Barre was the business center of the Wyoming Valley, then Ashley was literally where the dirty work took place, as evidenced by some of the early names attached to this working-class village: Peestone, Coalville, Scrabbletown and Skunktown, to name a few.

Ashley is also the site of the Huber Coal Breaker, a tall, imposing structure where large chunks of coal were literally broken into small pieces for easier shipping and sale. Breakers were easily identified from a distance because of their dark, coal-like color and sloped roofs. In its day, the

The Huber Breaker has been a monument to the anthracite industry since 1892.

Huber Breaker was one of the largest ever built, and the work force inside consisted of boys as young as 8 to 9 years old, and former miners who were either disabled or too old to work the mines. The old adage, "Twice a boy and once a man is the poor miner's life" referred to the two stints a miner spent in the breakers, interrupted by his "man" years in the mines. Regardless of age, everyone worked 10 hours a day, six days week, for 51 cents a week in 1884. At one point, one out of every four mine workers was a boy.

While not open to the public, the Huber Breaker is a monument to the region's robust past, and is visible from Interstate 81 and Route 309 in the Borough of Ashley.

The biggest challenge mining companies faced was getting

The Ashley Planes.

anthracite over the valley's confining ridges to the lucrative markets to the south. In an ingenious act of engineering and daring, the miners in the 1840s constructed a series of steep, inclined planes at Ashley. These planes rose 1,000 feet above the valley floor and were equipped with tracks, on which railroad-like coal cars coasted downhill by gravity, and empty cars were pulled back uphill by powerful stationary engines.

State Game Lands Trail Etiquette
Hike with caution

Some terrain alongside the D&L Trail is labeled "game lands." While "game" may suggest carefree fun and frolicking, in this case you need to exercise extreme caution because hunting is a prime activity.

Specifically, the D&L Trail will pass through State Game Lands No.119 in Luzerne County. State Game Lands also exist on both sides of the trail north of White Haven, and they abut Lehigh Gorge State Park.

1. Always wear fluorescent orange clothing so you'll be visible to hunters.
2. Plan ahead by checking hunting season dates.
3. BE AWARE! Stay on designated trails only.
4. No motorized vehicles are allowed.
5. Please do not feed the wildlife
6. If you carry it in, carry it out.
7. Be respectful to other trail users.
8. State Game Land trails are non-motorized multiple use paths, so expect to share the land with others.

State Game Lands offer important habitat and open space along the D&L.

Nescopeck State Park

With its picturesque, stream-laced valleys and dramatic mountainous landscape, Nescopeck is ideally suited for those who crave undeveloped, natural land.

Plans call for linkages to Lehigh Gorge and Hickory Run state parks. Meanwhile, you can enjoy the many species of rare plants, critical habitats, recreational opportunities, and environmental education programs offered here.

Nescopeck State Park hosts Pennsylvania's newest environmental education facility.

Eastern Middle Coal Field: Quarrying vs. Shaft Mining

The Eastern Middle Anthracite Field in Luzerne County is the smallest of the four Pennsylvania fields. It's made up of a series of narrow, parallel basins that rest on a high plateau. Because the coal outcrops are on ridgetops, instead of buried below the surface, quarrying or strip mining

was preferred. Strip mining continues today so you may encounter an enormous drag line operating in what looks like a moonscape. Look closely and you can see hardy aspens and birch trees taking root—evidence that the land is trying to return to its natural state.

-35-

White Haven
Where canal meets railroad, a community is born

The dam at White Haven was popular with local swimmers and created hydro-electric power.

and housed two railroad stations, a pair of hotels and various stores. The stations and passenger trains have long since vanished, but you can still hear the whistle of Reading, Blue Mountain & Northern Railroad freight trains passing through town. Railroad buffs journey to White Haven to see the restored, 29-ton, yellow, Union Pacific caboose that sits along South Main St., housing railroad memorabilia.

In the 1800s White Haven enjoyed the enviable status of being the point where canal met rail. Here, the Lehigh Canal began its southerly journey downstream to Easton, while the Lehigh & Susquehanna Railroad stretched north to Wilkes-Barre. Thanks to its status as a key link in the anthracite-shipping network, White Haven prospered. A visitor to town may have seen hundreds of railroad cars, laden with mountains of stone coal mined in the north and timber cut from White Haven's surrounding forests, all waiting to be transferred onto the Lehigh Canal's barges.

When a flood washed out the canal in 1862, the Lehigh Valley and Lehigh & Susquehanna Railroads raced to become the prime means of shipping goods and people. Following alongside the Lehigh River's banks were Lehigh & Susquehanna tracks leased to New Jersey Central Railroad. A block away was the Lehigh Valley Railroad. Main Street ran between the two

Named for Josiah White, co-founder of the Lehigh Coal and Navigation Co., the town today stands as the northern-most gateway to Lehigh Gorge State Park, and is best known for its rails-to-trails hiking and biking routes, whitewater rafting and paddling opportunities. To reach the White Haven Access Area, take Exit 273 on I-80. Follow PA 940 east to the Thriftway store, go through the parking lot, then bear left until you reach the parking area and trailhead on the Lehigh River.

By 1868, rail service was available between White Haven and Easton.

Hikes to try: To follow the D&L Trail south from White Haven, hop on the Lehigh Gorge Rail-Trail. It's about 26 miles and all downhill to Jim Thorpe.

Step-like cribbing fortifies the Upper Grand Lehigh Navigation System.

No. 28 and 29: Remnants of glorious locks

Lock No. 28 and 29 are very accessible high-lift locks located near the north and south ends of Main Street in White Haven. In their prime, these locks could raise and lower boats 25 feet—an impressive accomplishment for that era.

Attached to the right of the lock was a massive, stone abutment that was part of the rock-and-timber White Haven Dam. Also known as Dam # 20, it functioned from 1838 until it was deemed unsafe and destroyed by the Army Corps of Engineers in 1951. The formidable dam was 375 feet long and 75 feet high.

The scale of the high-lift locks is impressive.

Coincidentally, the island and alluvial flats upstream from the dam site are made of bottom deposits that piled up when a lake was created behind the dam.

Mining the Woodlands

In early days, immense stands of white pine, hemlock and oak thrived here. But as more settlers moved in seeking ways to make a living, many trees were cut and floated downriver to be used as mine props and lumber. Around 1800, the forests were being cut at a dramatic rate to supply domestic firewood, building materials, and charcoal for iron furnaces. Lumbering peaked around 1865 when timber operations expanded to satisfy growing city markets.

Eckley Miners' Village

In 1854, Eckley was a thriving "patch" town, one of several that mining companies built near coal fields to attract laborers. Eckley Cox and Asa Lansford Foster constructed this company town as cheaply and quickly as possible, with the coal and transport firms owning the houses, school, stores, streets, and even making and enforcing the laws. A man's ethnicity and status in the mine affected the size and location of his house.

Today Eckley Village is a museum that's listed as a National Register Historic District and operated by the Pennsylvania Historical & Museum Commission. Eckley's stark landscape was used as background for the filming of Paramount Studio's 1960s movie "The Molly Maguires," which was inspired by events that occurred in the region.

With its rich immigrant history and simple setting, you can walk Eckley's streets and become acquainted with life as it was for the many ethnic groups that lived and worked together in company towns.

For more information

For info on tours, resources, facilities, events, parks, golf courses and outdoor recreation contact: Luzerne County Convention and Visitor Bureau, Public Square, Wilkes-Barre, PA 18701; Call 888-905-2872 or visit www.tournepa.com.

Old World Influences
Immigrants shape the coal towns & give rise to the labor movement.

Look closely as you travel through Luzerne and Carbon Counties and you'll see telling reminders of the region's heritage: culm piles of unmarketable mining residue, rusty railroad tracks that once shined brightly from constant use, occasional remains of a strip mine. What's not immediately visible, though, is the immigrant-based population that thrived here, creating communities that were forged around such strong Old World traditions that their cultural influences are still vital today.

Because the mountainous counties were remote and without navigable roads or rivers, they stayed sparsely populated after adjoining areas were settled. That changed once coal was discovered and the transportation system developed. From the 1820s on, coal companies actively recruited miners and engineers from England, Scotland and Wales, anxious to adapt European technology to the American anthracite fields.

Irish laborers fleeing famine came to the minefields in the 1840-50s. Balkan and Polish people and Italians arrived in the 1860s and into the 20th century, driven from their homelands by famine, conscription and repression.

Catholic immigrants found that the earlier-arriving Protestants were running the new world and owned mines, transportation systems, housing and stores, and held the best paying, most skilled jobs. As a result, late-arriving Irish and Eastern Europeans suffered religious, ethnic and labor discrimination.

To combat oppressive conditions, the Catholics developed strong ethnic and religious communities centered on their parishes. Fraternal societies and strong adherence to their culture resulted, as did labor unions created to prevent exploitation of the miners.

Carbon County
The D&L Trail's Mecca for outdoor recreation

Breathtaking scenery, natural lakes, a free-flowing river, abundant wildlife, and the remnants of the coal and lumber industries coexist in this mountainous region widely known as a Mecca for quality outdoor recreation. River rafting, mountain biking, kayaking, canoeing, hiking, hunting, camping, fishing, golfing, downhill and cross country skiing—you can do as much or as little as your heart (and muscles) desire, thanks to the variety of resorts, state game lands, rail-trails, and state, county and municipal parks scattered along this section of the D&L Trail.

Towns are few and small. They stand as reminders of an economy that grew from their importance to transportation and small-scale agriculture. This remains the most undeveloped region the D&L Trail passes through. Today it's largely state game, forest and park land. In some locations, Carbon County is still as wild as when John James Audubon sketched birds here more than 200 years ago.

The Appalachian Mountains and Pocono Plateau converge here so you can enjoy spectacular views of long green valleys and wooded slopes. Backwoods are laced with ponds and wetlands, all left behind by passing Ice Age glaciers. Three state parks and thousands of acres of State Game Lands protect many of the mountain ridges from development. All total, more than 100,000 acres are publicly owned.

Carbon County is a wonderland for outdoor enthusiasts. Wildflowers cover former industrial land. Hikers have replaced canal boats.

Audubon's legacy, in his own words
Recorded auto tour brings the artist and father of conservation alive.

Red-tailed Hawks are found in woods with open land and high perches nearby.

In 1829, naturalist John James Audubon spent six weeks in a wooded, mountainous section of the Lehigh River Valley then known as the Great Pine Forest. As a guest of the logging field boss for the Lehigh Coal and Navigation Co, Audubon cataloged and sketched many of the bird species found on the company-owned acreage, which was thick with mostly virgin white pine and hemlock.

But as Audubon watched the rate at which the timber was being harvested (to build coal arks and generate income), he became concerned about the future health of the woodlands. He wrote:

"Trees one after another were, and are yet, constantly heard falling during the days; and in calm nights, the greedy saw mills told a sad tale, that in a century the noble forests should exist no more. Many mills were erected, many dams raised, in defiance of the impetuous Lehigh. One full third of the trees have already been culled, turned into boards and floated as far as Philadelphia."

The extensive clear cutting did have serious consequences. The great flood

Great Blue Herons grow to nearly four feet tall and are common at the edges of the Lehigh River and Canal.

Like John J. Audubon, you will discover the region's beauty.

of 1862 that destroyed dams on the Lehigh River and helped end the region's canal era was caused by massive runoff on land that had no trees or vegetation to absorb the excessive rainfall.

Numerous groups work to protect the Lehigh River.

Today, the land where Audubon planted the seeds for his life-long preservation ethic has healed. You can see for yourself on the Audubon Auto Tour, a prerecorded, taped presentation that retraces his journey through Jim Thorpe, Weatherly, Rockport and White Haven. "Exploring Audubon's Lehigh" carries you 53 miles through valley towns and some of the finest scenery nature has to offer. The tour takes 3-6 hours to complete, with 12 stops on the primary tour route and 6 suggested side trips, including a mining village, a lake resort, and a sea of boulders. For more info or to purchase tapes contact: Exploring Audubon's Lehigh, P.O. Box 134, Weatherly, PA 18255, www.audubonslehigh.org.

The ruins at Lehigh Tannery are evidence of past productivity.

The standing remains of Locks # 29, 28, 23, 8,7 and 2 are also visible today, as are the 600-foot stone ruins of the old Lehigh Tannery. Vats and walls have also been uncovered by D&L Trail Tenders, who volunteer their time to help ongoing preservation efforts.

By 1841, 38 sawmills stood on the banks of the Lehigh River between White Haven and Jim Thorpe. Most of the river's tributaries were dammed to provide water for mills and to create ponds to hold the logs until they could be floated to market via the Lehigh. Bark from hemlock trees yielded tannin for curing leather, which grew to become an important riverside industry. By 1855, the village of Lehigh Tannery was the nation's second largest producer of tanned hides.

The stone rubble remnants of Lock No. 27 are near the old Lehigh Tannery site. Also known as "the Pennsylvania," this lock could raise and lower boats over 30 feet—an impressive achievement 150 years ago.

Lehigh Tannery is an additional access for the Lehigh Gorge.

Diverse wild areas, plus unique geological formations make Hickory Run an excellent outdoor classroom.

If not for a lot of ice that once passed through, this magnificent acreage might be a farm instead of one of the premier parks in Pennsylvania.

The first humans to explore the area now known as Hickory Run State Park found dark forests thick with evergreens, swamps and bogs. Lenni Lenape, Susquehannock and Iroquois Indians traveled through, but there were no known settlements. Part of the reason is the ground; Ice Age glaciers once covered half of what now constitutes the park, leaving behind poor soil too rocky to farm.

During the American Revolution, British and Indian allies routed American forces at the Battle of Wyoming and some refugees fled through the swamps and dark forests. The huge tree growth made the area dark and poor drainage caused it to be menacing, hence gaining the name, "Shades of Death."

By 1829 the Lehigh Canal was complete and the region experienced boom times. By 1839 six mills were operating and a stagecoach road connecting Allentown and Wilkes-Barre came through the area. The road gave rise to the town of Saylorsville just north of Hickory Run. Today the route is known as the Stage Trail, where some foundations from the town remain.

The Lehigh River flows along the western boundary of Hickory Run State Park.

Between 1890 and 1918 floods and fires ravaged the land. In 1918, Allentown millionaire General Harry C. Trexler started buying up acreage and said, "I would like to see Hickory Run developed into a state park where families can come and enjoy wholesome recreation." He opened the land to public hunting and fishing, and fenced off 1,000 acres to raise game animals. Wardens patrolled the propagation area, and part of the path they routinely walked is today's Gamewire Trail.

After 1935, the National Park Service purchased Hickory Run. In 1945 it was transferred to the Commonwealth of Pennsylvania and Hickory Run State Park was born.

A sea of boulders

Hickory Run's Boulder Field is a National Natural Landmark, and is exactly what its name suggests. The flat, barren field is roughly 400' x 1,800', with the boulder layer about 10 feet thick. Some rocks are 26 feet long, but most are less than 4 feet in length.

The stark vastness of Boulder Field is remarkable.

Bears: Cute and cunning

They look cuddly but the size and strength of local black bears is astonishing. They can climb a tree like a raccoon, horn or banging a pot to chase it away. Never approach a bear, and be especially careful of a mother and her cubs. Notify park employees if you have difficulties with bears.

There are 23 hiking trails at Hickory Run.

A smorgasbord of recreational activities

Directions and information on hiking, swimming, camping, picnicking, group tenting, group cabin rentals, hunting, fishing, cross-country skiing, ice skating, snowmobiling, and access for people with disabilities can be found at:

Hickory Run State Park
RR #1, Box 81
White Haven, PA 18661-9712
570-443-0400
e-mail: hickoryrunsp@state.pa.us
www.dcnr.state.pa.us

Bear cubs are sent up trees when mom senses danger.

run as fast as a race horse, and eat plants, grasses, berries, occasionally meat, and human food whenever available. Their claws are designed to tear apart rotting logs to find food, but also help bears open garbage cans and coolers (store all food and coolers in your vehicle with the windows rolled up). Most bears will avoid humans, but can be aggressive if you come between them and food. If this happens, try yelling, honking the car

Mountain biking is permitted in nearby Lehigh Gorge State Park.

The spectacular gorge that lends its name to this State Park slices through the Pocono Plateau for nearly 26 miles, creating a dramatic landscape of steep, hemlock- and rhododendron-covered slopes, rocky escarpments, and side streams that surge into waterfalls. The 4,548-acre park follows the Lehigh River from the U.S. Army Corps of Engineers' Francis E. Walter Dam at the north, to Jim Thorpe at the southern end.

The towering, 800-foot Gorge was carved into the plateau by the Lehigh River. It is a

Numerous streams, like Indian Run at Rockport, flow into the Lehigh River.

Licensed outfitters provide everything needed for paddling the Lehigh.

Follow U.S. 209 south to Jim Thorpe. Take PA 903 north across the river to Coalport Road. Turn off Coalport Road to access Glen Onoko.

Rockport Access area: To reach the central access area from the south, follow US 209 south from Jim Thorpe to PA 93 north, continuing to SR 2055 (Lehigh Gorge Drive), through Weatherly into the small village of Rockport at SR 4014.

From the north, follow PA 940 west from Exit 273 off I-80, left onto SR 2055 (Lehigh Gorge Drive), continuing to the village of Rockport at SR 4014.

White Haven Access Area: The northern access area can be reached off Exit 273 on I-80. Follow PA 940 east to the Thriftway store, go through the parking lot and bear left to the state park access area.

Lehigh Gorge State Park
c/o Hickory Run State Park
RR #1, Box 81
White Haven, PA 18661-9712
570-443-0400
e-mail: hickoryrunsp@state.pa.us
www.dcnr.state.pa.us

designated state scenic river and the lure for many outdoor lovers. They travel here for the whitewater, and the bucking-bronco sensation that comes when barreling over rapids and paddling down a swift-moving river. Bicyclists come for the uninterrupted 26 mile trail that travels downhill from White Haven to Jim Thorpe along the Lehigh. Inexperienced boaters should not attempt the Lehigh. If you're unsure of your abilities, outfitted trips are available from licensed concessionaires who provide rafts, guides, all safety equipment and transport to and from the river.

Getting there

Glen Onoko Access Area: The southern access point can be reached by taking Exit 74, Northeast Extension, Pennsylvania Turnpike.

The 15-mile stretch between White Haven and Penn Haven Junction is open to snowmobiles.

Rockport

A railroad town with park and trail access

In 1819, the Lehigh Coal & Navigation Company (LC&N) purchased rich timber holdings in the area around what is now the village of Rockport. The company built four sawmills along Indian, Laurel, and Leslie Run. Over the ensuing decades, more saw and grist mills sprang up on other tributary streams in the Lehigh Gorge.

A bike ride from Rockport to Jim Thorpe or White Haven takes about 1-1/2 to 3 hours.

Today you'll find one of the oldest (ca. 1838-40) and smallest hard-rock railroad tunnels here. It was part of the Buck Mountain Gravity Railroad system.

In 1884, the Lehigh Valley Railroad's final tunnel in Pennsylvania was completed. Known as the Rockport Tunnel, it's one of the longest (1100'), active tunnels along the line and is located about one mile east of town on the west side of the Lehigh River.

at Leslie Run. Southbound, heading toward Jim Thorpe, a bridge crosses over the Black Creek and then you'll traverse Penn Haven/Independence Junction (about half way between the two towns). Various railroad lines met here and had the option of switching track direction. These are active railroad tracks—***use caution!***

Hikes to try: This is the area where you'll start to sense the depth of the gorge. When you head north out of Rockport on the D&L Trail, keep an eye open for the falls

Jim Thorpe

Millionaires, coal-car roller coasters, and a touch of Switzerland in the lair of the bear

Jim Thorpe's main street is part of a National Historic District.

Jim Thorpe stands as a shining example of resilience and fortitude, having withstood the loss of the coal industry and hard economic times in the ensuing years. The settlement that was arguably the linchpin in the canal-and-rail system—the D&L "capital," if you will—is thriving again.

The town that today carries the name of a legendary Native American athlete was established in 1818 as Mauch Chunk, which means "Bear Mountain" and

refers to the shape of the neighboring mountainside. Entrepreneurs led by

The shape of Bear Mountain provided the inspiration for naming Mauch Chunk.

The picturesque landscape at Jim Thorpe inspired early artists.

sions, as well, and prestigious churches overlooked town. Elegant townhouses built along Broadway became known as Millionaires Row.

Around 1923 with coal mining all but a memory, Mauch Chunk saw an economic decline. A potential solution arose in 1954 when Mauch Chunk and East Mauch Chunk merged to form the Borough of Jim Thorpe. The name change occurred when Patricia Thorpe, widow of famed American Indian athlete Jim Thorpe, was visiting nearby Philadelphia. She heard about the two towns' efforts to merge, traveled to Mauch Chunk, and suggested that if the newly-joined towns would adopt her late husband's name and pro-

Josiah White and Erskine Hazard formed the LC&N here in the 1820s, and shipped countless tons of anthracite coal and other goods to market via the Lehigh and Delaware Canals. The town grew in importance when it was named Carbon County's seat in 1843.

In the 1850s, Asa Packer financed the Lehigh Valley Railroad and reliance on canals began to diminish. Because Mauch Chunk was a prominent transfer point, the railroad triggered a period of prosperity as it carried industrial goods to market. The rail line also made access easy, so the town became an excursion destination for tourists. Thanks to the grandeur of the Lehigh River Gorge, surrounding steep, wooded hillsides, its quaint, narrow streets and terraced gardens, Mauch Chunk earned the nickname "the Switzerland of America" and attracted artists intrigued by the scenery and Victorian architecture.

Between 1850-90, construction boomed. In 1861, Packer, who went on to establish Lehigh University, built a hillside mansion overlooking town. Youngest son Harry's mansion, a wedding gift from his parents, was built next door. Other industrialists built mountainside man-

The Asa Packer Mansion is one of Jim Thorpe's two National Historic Landmarks.

Race Street is home to several local artists.

When In Jim Thorpe: Landmarks and Sites to See

There are many Victorian-era gems to see in "Old Mauch Chunk." A few you should not miss include two National Historic Landmarks. The Asa Packer Mansion was the hillside home of the millionaire and founder of the Lehigh Valley Railroad. It has been preserved with the Packer Family's original furnishings. St. Mark's Episcopal Church, the Packer family place of worship is also open to the public.

The Mauch Chunk Opera House presents live theater and music. The Mauch Chunk Museum features local memorabilia and scale models of the Switchback Railroad and Lehigh Canal. The Old Carbon County Jail's most famous occupants were the Molly Maguires, the elusive Irish miner organization seeking bet-

vide a stately mausoleum for his remains, great rewards would befall the town. Jim Thorpe's mausoleum is located along Route 903.

Town officials began an intensive revitalization effort in the mid-1970s. The result was the establishment of the Old Mauch Chunk National Historic District, where the ornately designed 19th century buildings reflect the town's wealth during the Victorian era. Today, the town's narrow streets are lined with shops, galleries, museums, restaurants and bed and breakfasts.

Jim Thorpe Area Chamber of Commerce
P.O. Box 164
Jim Thorpe, PA 18229
1-888-Jim-Thorpe
www.jimthorpe.org

Old Mauch Chunk Landing
Pocono Mountains Vacation Bureau
Visitors Center
570-325-3673

Visitor Information is available in the Old Mauch Chunk Landing in the RR Station.

ter working conditions. One condemned man supposedly left a hand print on his cell wall as testimony of his innocence. Asa Packer Park has as its centerpiece a 15,000-pound chunk of anthracite that came from Panther Valley. Finally, the D&L Landing and Visitor Information Center is housed within the former N.J. Central Railroad Passenger Station. It's a focal point in this small town, and bustles with special events, exhibits, festivals and seasonal train rides.

The trip between the mines at Summit Hill and the Lehigh Canal was nine miles, one way. On the downhill section, gravity-pulled coal cars reached speeds of up to 50 mph. From its inception, tourists could ride the Switchback when no coal was being hauled, resulting in modern boasts that it was America's first roller coaster.

The Switchback has renewed life as a recreational trail.

Hikes to try: The Switchback was retired as coal carrier in 1871, and became solely a tourist attraction. It still is today, attracting those who want to hike, bike or cross-country ski along its path. The Switchback Trail is a federally-designated National Recreation Trail that runs from Jim Thorpe to Summit Hill for 16 miles (round-trip).

Coal cars and tourists were pulled up Mount Pisgah to descend the Switchback Railroad.

Anthracite was mined in the Summit Hill high country. The river and Canals to ship it to market were down below in Mauch Chunk. How to get coal to boats?

In 1827, the Switchback Gravity Railroad was devised. By 1844, it consisted of railroad track, cars, and steep, inclined planes where the rail line headed downhill to carry empty cars back to the mines in Summit Hill. The Switchback was the nation's first commercially successful and permanent railroad.

Mountain Laurel blossoms in mid-June.

Summit Hill

The story of the "Stone Coal Way" literally begins here, where Philip Ginder in 1791 discovered a black rock that turned out to be stone coal, or anthracite. A memorial to Ginder is located in Ludlow Park to honor the man who received a small tract of land as compensation for his discovery.

The first commercial link between the coal region and a seaport was due to the discovery of anthracite.

In 1859 a burning, underground mine was discovered at the west end of Summit Hill. Despite the community's best view surface cracks that emitted steam, smoke, and occasionally flames. Patches of grass stayed green in winter due to the warmth from below.

For information on any of these sites, contact the Summit Hill Historical Society at 570-645-3634. The Society's Museum features displays of the area's history, and is located

Although long-gone, Summit Hill's Switchback Station was an early tourist destination.

efforts to extinguish the blaze, it smoldered until 1941. The mine eventually became a tourist attraction as visitors would get off the Switchback Railroad to at 12 East Ludlow Street. The Museum is open Fridays 4-7 p.m., other times by appointment.

Lansford

Lansford's cultural patchwork is found amidst its places of worship.

This town's turning point was 1870-71, when a railroad tunnel was cut through Nesquehoning Mountain, linking the Panther and Hauto Valleys. This achievement meant coal from Panther Valley could be easily transported by rail to Mauch Chunk through the Hauto Tunnel, without first having to be shipped up the mountain planes via gravity railroad to Summit Hill. This simpler, more efficient transportation link prompted the Lehigh Navigation Coal Company to move its main offices to Lansford. And wherever the Company went, attention followed.

The village of Andrewsville at the east end of Lansford Borough remains a good example of a company-built "patch town." These villages were hastily built by mine owners to house miners and their families. The goal was simple: fit as many people into one area as possible. By doing so, the result was tremendous ethnic diversity, often with five different cultures living on the same street, comparing and sharing ways of life. Unfortunately, houses were often built on unstable grounds over mines, outhouses were near water supplies and helped spread disease and illness, the rent was usually high, and conditions in general were crowded and cramped.

This cultural diversity also led to a wide array of landmark churches. The Lansford Historical Society has a self-guided tour available.

No. 9 Mine and Museum: Today you can ride by rail 1,600 feet underground and take a walking tour of a mine's innermost workings. While in the deep shaft, originally opened in 1855, you can explore muleways (narrow underground passages connecting different tunnels) and view a miner's hospital room cut in solid stone.

No. 9 Mine & Museum
9 Dock Street
Lansford, PA 18232
570-645-7074
http://no9mine.tripod.com

A great collection of anthracite artifacts can be found at Lansford's No. 9 Museum.

Molly Maguire Auto Tour

Saints or criminals? You decide on this self-guided excursion.

In the 1870s the anthracite fields were the scene of continued violence, and a group of Irishmen known as the Molly Maguires were blamed. To mine owners, they were a secret society bent on murder and sabotage. To miners, they were mysterious avengers trying to force owners to improve working conditions.

After a particularly bitter and violent series of strikes between miners and "company men," several alleged Molly Maguires were accused of murder and held in the Carbon County Jail. They died on the jail's gallows in 1877 and 1878.

The Molly Maguire saga isn't just a story of intimidation and violence. It's also a tale of the hard, dangerous life coal miners endured, as well as the abuse they experienced at the hands of financial titans.

To get a taste of this lawless era you can take the Molly Maguire Auto Tour, which is a self-guided, round-trip loop beginning at either the Jim Thorpe Train Station (Delaware & Lehigh National Heritage Corridor Landing and Visitors Center) or the Schuylkill County Visitors Bureau at the Quality Hotel in Pottsville, PA.

An audio tape and accompanying booklet with map can be purchased at both locations. The tour carries you through Carbon and Schuylkill counties. It takes three to eight hours, depending on your pace.

Old Mauch Chunk Landing
Pocono Mountains Vacation
Bureau Visitors Center
Railroad Station
Jim Thorpe, PA 18229
570-325-3673

Schuylkill County Visitors Bureau
Quality Hotel
200 East Arch Street
Pottsville, PA 17901
570-622-7700
www.schuylkill.org

Panther Valley
The historical and industrial transition zone

One legend holds that this valley was named for the abundance of sleek, stealthy and rather large cats that prowled the woodlands and mountains when the first settlers arrived. Then there are those ol' timers who say the area was named in part for the small upper valley of the westward-flowing Panther Creek.

Either way, the Panther Valley lies between two deeper valleys formed by Nesquehoning and Mauch Chunk creeks, both of which flow east to the Lehigh River. The result is a geographic transition zone, where the Lehigh River emerges from the Lehigh Gorge and cuts across the last of the Appalachian Mountain ridges.

This is also a historical and industrial transition zone, where events unfolded that changed the way both U.S. industry and organized labor go about their business. The valley was home to the first permanent, commercially successful railroad in the United States, and the site of the first successful anthracite mine (at Summit Hill). Its unofficial capital, Lansford was home to the powerful Lehigh Navigation Coal Company. Jim Thorpe (formerly Mauch Chunk) served as the transfer point for resources mined in the narrow Panther Valley.

Panther Valley Anthracite Auto Tour
The easiest way to understand this land of sweat and opportunity

Panther Valley is a place where men with great wealth lived close to miners whose greatest assets were their strong backs. Immigrants from distant lands settled and created strongly-knit communities that still flourish today. It's a land of sweat and toil, and of opportunity and reward.

Taking the self-guided Panther Valley Anthracite Auto Tour is one of the best ways to see and appreciate the region's historical and cultural offerings. You take your own vehicle and go at your own pace. The Tour includes Jim Thorpe, Nesquehoning, Lansford, Coaldale, Tamaqua, and Summit Hill. These key towns all have a part in the anthracite story.

Tour highlights include the many historic buildings in Jim Thorpe; the

mine stables and mine car memorial in Nesquehoning; a mining patch town in Lansford; the miner's hospital in Coaldale; and the Ginder Monument in Summit Hill.

Tour booklets are available at the Visitors Center in Jim Thorpe, as well as at the No. 9 Mine & Museum.

FROM JIM THORPE
TO EASTON

Industry Unfolds Along the Lehigh River,
Shaping the Land and People

Family-run farms co-exist beside heavy industry in the Lehigh Valley.

Hike the D&L Trail north to south and just past Jim Thorpe you'll notice a distinct change in land's character. The thickly-wooded, mountainous terrain gives way to a pastoral landscape. Mines, breakers, patch towns and other telltale signs of the coal industry are replaced by covered bridges, mid-18th century German villages, elegant Victorian houses, and the rolling fields of Pennsylvania German farms. The land here is productive, but in a different way.

You're now entering the Lehigh Valley, the heart of the D&L Trail, where the most intensive urbanization and industri-

Bethlehem Steel supplied armies, navies, built cities and employed thousands.

The Lehigh River—water, transportation, power and natural beauty.

alization occurred, both past and present. In its industrial heyday, the Valley was the center of the region's economic strength. Slate, zinc and limestone for cement were processed here, while iron and steel dominated local economies and impacted events around the world.

This impact created distinctly different industrial and cultural communities, such as Walnutport and Slatington, which existed purely because of the Lehigh Canal and railroads. A bit farther south, the region's three largest cities—Allentown, Bethlehem and Easton— became the cradle of the American Industrial Revolution in large part because of the canal.

The Lehigh Valley has numerous towns and cities with distinct histories, but in the context of the D&L Trail, it's all one big landscape where the urban, agricultural and natural lands found alongside the trail are linked by a coal transporting route that started in the mountains and fueled dramatic change on its way to market.

19th century influences create the ambience of Lehigh Valley communities.

For more information

For information on tours, attractions, seasonal activities parks and festivals, please contact the Lehigh Valley Convention & Visitors Bureau, PO Box 20785, Lehigh Valley, PA 18002-0785. Call: 800-747-0561 E-mail: geninfo@lehighvalleypa.org Website: www.lehighvalleypa.org.

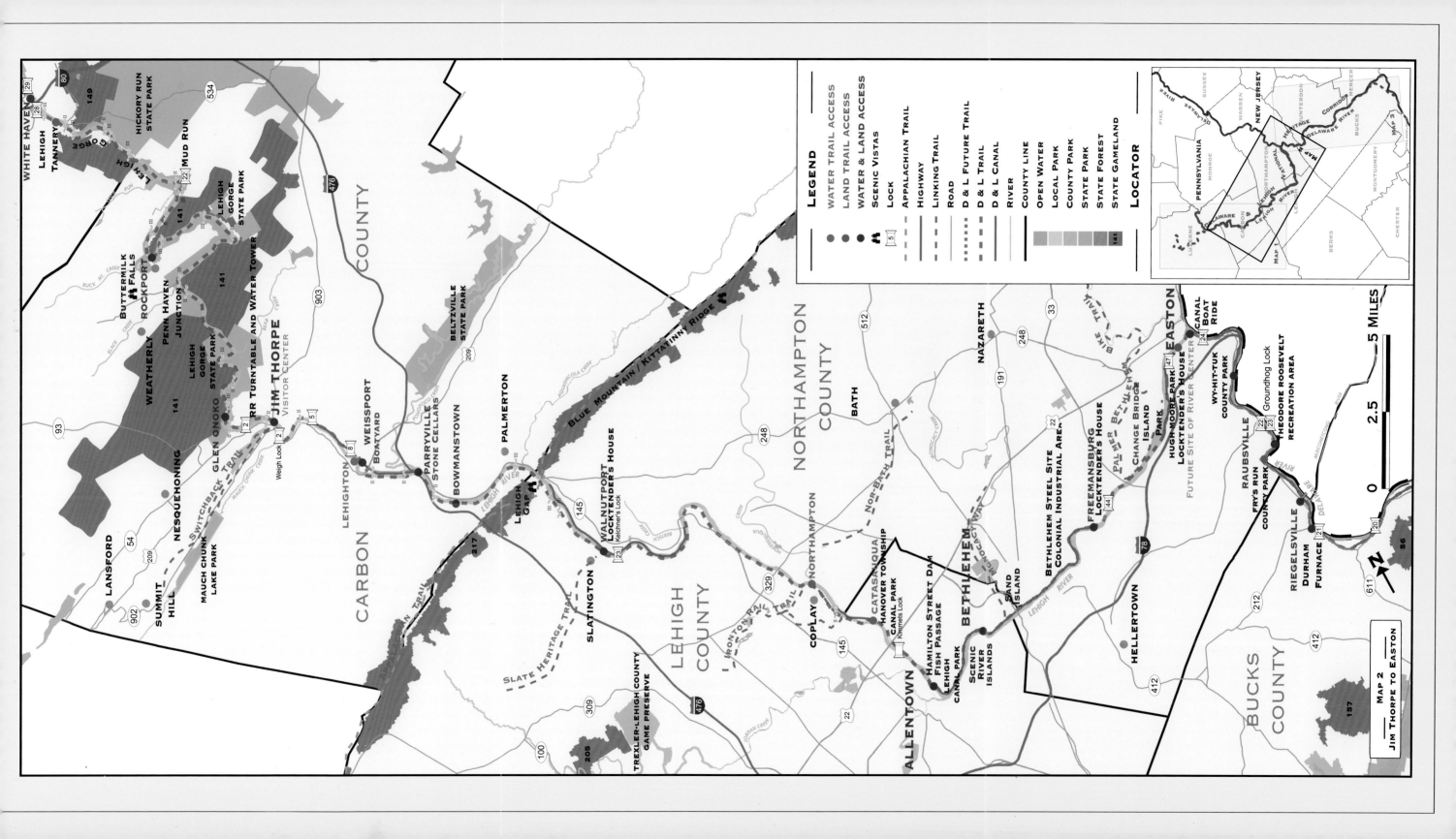

MAP 2
JIM THORPE TO EASTON

The first humans to settle in the Lehigh Valley were paleo-Indians, but the best known are the Lenni Lenape (meaning "real" or "original people") of the Delaware Nation. Roughly 5,000 Lenape lived here in the early 17th century, occupying a territory that stretched from the Delaware Bay to the Blue (Kittatiny) Mountain, and from the Atlantic Coast to the Delaware-Susquehanna watershed. Many came from nearby territory— today's New Jersey.

Lehigh Valley was of great importance because it was one of their main east-west pathways, plus it intersected with major north-south aboriginal trails in the Delaware Valley. Despite its prominence as a

In the early 1600s, Lenape ancestors were among the first Native Americans to come in contact with Europeans.

The Lenape way of life centered on the Delaware Valley (Bucks County), where they hunted deer, grew grains and vegetables, and caught seafood along the coast. The

crossroads, the "Great Valley" as they referred to the area, was the site of few permanent villages, although they often camped at the confluence of the Lehigh and Delaware rivers at what's now Easton.

The first Europeans in the Lehigh Valley were Scots-Irish who followed Saucon and Indian creeks and established settlements in today's Northampton County. The first was known as the Craig settlement,

< *Please open to Delaware & Lehigh National Heritage Corridor Map 2—Jim Thorpe to Easton*

Tours are available at the 1756 Troxell-Steckel Homestead in Egypt.

named after the most prominent pioneer family. In 1730 a second, smaller cluster of wilderness farms became known as the Hunter Settlement, named for early pioneer leader Alexander Hunter.

Large numbers of Germans came into the Lehigh Valley in the 1730s, most of them Protestant farmers and members of the Lutheran and Reformed faith. Among them were the Schwenkfelders (from Saxony) and Mennonites, known for their skills as craftsmen and millers, and for establishing well respected schools. Most of the Germans became known as Pennsylvania Dutch, or Pennsylvania Germans. They grew maize, squash, and wheat in the fertile soils, and took great care of their livestock. They also took pride in the impressive barns they built, a style the English soon adapted.

White settlers and the Lenape generally got along fine. The Indians had an

especially warm relationship with Pennsylvania founding father William Penn. That all changed when his sons

Local historical societies keep the history of the Valley's "first people" alive.

instigated the infamous 1737 Walking Purchase, which swindled the Lenape out of hundreds of square miles of prime hunting territory. Relations became strained and the Lenape were eventually driven west and northward, where they and the Iroquois became pawns between the French, English and colonists in the French and Indian Wars of the 1740s. By 1765, most of the remaining Indians had migrated from the region.

grew a unique and broad cultural environment in which music, art and education flourished, as did religious tolerance. Their massive communal dwellings, churches and industrial structures remain today as landmarks in Bethlehem and Nazareth.

The success of the American Revolution inspired many oppressed Europeans to view the U.S. as a place of freedom and opportunity. This factor, coupled with the iron and coal industries' insatiable demand for laborers, triggered an influx of immigrant workers in the early 1800s. At least 50 different nations and ethnic groups have been identified among the immigrants of the nineteenth century, and their descendants still

Quilting was thought to be a passing fad in the 1800s. Today it is recognized as an important social ritual and art form.

With the Indians gone from their traditional lands, German settlements in the Valley swelled. Among the most important arrivals were the Moravians. They were a communal sect that developed highly organized towns in which each resident had a prescribed role, everyone contributed to the settlement's well being, and all were taken care of in time of need.

To live in a Moravian settlement, you had to be a full member of the Church. However they believed all men to be equal, so their cemeteries held Germans, Irish, Indians and those of African descent. From these beginnings there

live in the Lehigh Valley.

Completion of the Lehigh Canal further accelerated development of the Valley. Suddenly transportation was easier. Entrepreneurs used it in combination with abundant raw materials, capital, labor and land to carry out unprecedented industrialization and urbanization. Many European immigrants arriving at New York's Ellis Island traveled straight to the Lehigh Valley, and by the late 1800s had turned Allentown, Bethlehem and Easton into the large, thriving cities you see today as you stroll along the D&L Trail.

Lehighton

From Indian Wars to a peaceful, riverside settlement

The Lenni Lenape were converted to Christianity through baptism by Moravian missionaries.

The look and character of Lehighton reflect its German ancestry; some 58 percent of the residents have German roots.

This small town began when the Moravian Brethren started converting the local Lenape Indians to Christianity. In 1746, the Moravians organized a mission in what is now Lehighton, and named it Gnadenhutten (meaning "tents of grace"). As the settlement grew, missionaries established another village along the east side of the river and named it New Gnadenhutten (today's Weissport).

The Delaware and Moravians lived peacefully in these settlements. In 1750, Teedyuscung,

who would become a great diplomat, was even baptized as a Christian. Eventually, Teedyuscung felt his people were being treated unfairly by other whites in the area, so the Delaware joined forces with the Shawnees and prepared for war. Despite the pending danger, the Moravians stayed in Gnadenhutten. In late 1755, the mission was attacked, 10 people were killed, one was captured, and all buildings burned to the ground. New Gnadenhutten settlers, warned of the attack, were able to escape to Bethlehem.

Following the massacre, many forts were built along Blue Mountain, the most

Lehighton was founded as a Moravian settlement.

A spacious town park is Lehighton's centerpiece.

important being Fort Allen in present day Weissport. It was constructed by Benjamin Franklin and his men. It wasn't until after the Revolutionary War that settlers felt safe from Indian attacks. In 1794, war veteran Jacob Weiss and gun maker William Henry II owned most of the land on which Lehighton rests today. The settlement that arose, named after the Lehigh River, became a popular rest stop for those traveling along the road from Berwick to Easton. Taverns to refresh the weary travelers popped up, as did a tannery, general store, and a grist-mill in the early 1800s. The Moravians opened the first school in 1820.

Still, it wasn't until the Lehigh Canal was completed in 1829 that Lehighton began to grow and thrive. The building of the Lehigh Valley Railroad helped increase population. The town became one of the area's largest employers with the Packerton Yards repair shops nearby. Other businesses included the Lehigh Stove and Manufacturing Company, Lehighton Lace, the Lehighton Shirt Factory, and the Baer Silk Mill, which still stands today. Many churches and a synagogue were also built in the 1800s, still existing today. The Borough was incorporated in 1866.

Weissport
Easy trail access, plus Ben Franklin's well and fort

The little town of Weissport has several claims to fame. First, it's a great access point for the D&L Trail. Here you can easily slip onto the restored towpath and bike, hike, x-c ski or fish to your heart's content. The trail extends north to Jim Thorpe (about 4 miles) and south to Parryville (about 3 miles).

Second, the village sits on the site of Fort Allen, which was constructed by

The Henry Rickert House served as a local distribution center.

The towpath and canal remnants make a great "classroom" for local history.

Benjamin Franklin and his men in January 1756 in response to a series of Indian attacks. The fort's original well is a local landmark.

Third, Weissport served as a major building site for many of the boats used on the canal. Boat construction began here as early as the 1830s. The town's early development was greatly influenced by the Lehigh Canal's 1829 opening.

Nestled between the Lehigh Canal and River, Weissport has withstood its share of floods over the years. Despite the damaging high waters, many buildings from the early days have survived. So have the tracks for the old Central Railroad of New Jersey, which ran parallel to the canal. The line is still used today as part of the Norfolk Southern Railroad.

With the demise of the Lehigh Canal, textiles became the major industry from the early 1900s through the 1930s. In fact, more people worked in the mills than lived in the town.

While the Lehigh River has shaped a host of towns along its banks, in Parryville a small creek that feeds into the Lehigh had just as significant an impact on the people and economy.

It was along Pohopoco Creek around 1830 that Daniel Parry, president of the Pine Forest Lumber Company, built the first of several sawmills. The settlement grew around the mills and the town, named for Parry, eventually incorporated as a borough in 1874.

In 1855, the Carbon Iron Company opened and became Parryville's primary industry, employing several hundred people by the 1880s.

The Parryville dam produced large blocks of ice for refrigeration that were harvested during winter months.

As for the Lehigh Canal's influences on the town, Lock No. 13 became a major coal loading facility for the Beaver

Cold cellars kept local brews cool for transport downstream.

Meadow Railroad when it was built in 1836. After only a few years, the railroad bridge over the Lehigh River was destroyed by a devastating flood and never rebuilt. When the coal era ended, the canal continued serving local lumber companies. Elsewhere, the LC&N housed boat-towing canal mules in a large barn just south of town.

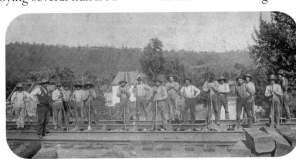

Hard working immigrants built the railroad infrastructure.

Just across the Lehigh River, the 4,461-foot Lehigh Tunnel is visible. This man-made wonder opened in the late 1950s, and a second tunnel was constructed in 1991 to handle the increasing traffic on the Pennsylvania Turnpike.

Bowmanstown

Paint steals the spotlight from coal in this community

The Locktender's House and related structures were found at each canal lock.

If coal yielded the Lehigh Canal, then Bowmanstown owes a share of its existence to paint. Or an ore used to make paint, to be precise.

Around 1855, Henry Bowman, Jr. discovered in nearby Stony Ridge a rock containing iron. When burned, it produced ochre, an excellent material for making reddish-brown protective paints. He soon started manufacturing ochre metallic red paint in its dry state—colors ranged from light ochre to dark Spanish brown—under the name of the Carbon Metallic Paint Works. Bowman's paint ore business grew and evolved, and the company reorganized and changed names several times over the years.

The town dates back to 1796, when farmer and lumberman John D. Bowman, Sr. settled here. Over the years, the village has been called Bowmansville and finally, Bowmanstown. Sand quarrying was also once a staple of this community.

In 1879, businessman Robert Prince moved his paint ore business to what was then known as Bowman's Station, the name reflecting the influence railroads had on small villages that sprang up along the tracks. Today the Prince Manufacturing Co., with its red-painted buildings, carries on this long tradition.

The town was the site of Lehigh Canal Lock No. 15, which was moved to accommodate the building of Route 248.

Veteran Lehigh River paddlers know of Bowmanstown for another reason: the waters near the lowhead dam make canoeing dangerous, and force recreational boaters to portage—that is, carry their canoes—around the obstruction.

Autumn is magnificent along the Lehigh.

45 MINUTES: How long it took well-trained mechanics and carpenters to build a coal ark. Since navigation at first was downstream only, the wooden arks were taken apart in Philadelphia and the lumber sold for housing construction. Raft men then walked or rode back to Mauch Chunk. As anthracite shipments increased, the need for more arks put a tremendous strain on the forests upstream. The LC&N eventually had to buy timberland to build arks.

22' X 100': Early lock size for the Lehigh Canal, identical to the measurements of the original Chesapeake and Delaware canals.

49: Number of locks in the Lehigh Canal system.

8: Number of dams, made of timber and stone with stone abutments.

LESS THAN 2 YEARS: Time it took, using scoops pulled by horses and mules, and men with picks, shovels and wheelbarrows, to complete the lower Lehigh Canal.

4 A.M. – 10 P.M.: Roughly, the boating hours on the Lehigh Canal; 6 days a week; season ran from the end of March until about the second week of December, when canal waters froze.

BOAT CREWS: 2 people, a captain and a mule driver; the crew and families lived in a tiny stern cabin and the 2 mules were stabled at the locks.

95 TONS: Average combined cargo capacity of canal boats when hauling coal downstream. Boats were weighed at Lock 2 just around the bend of the Lehigh River below Jim Thorpe. The water was drained so boats would rest on the scales.

HINGED BOAT: Most common type of boat used; 87.5 feet long x 10.5 feet wide; there was a small 8x10 foot cabin in the stern.

Palmerton
From zinc smelting to traditional Small Town USA

To understand Palmerton's past and why it exists today, think zinc. Palmerton was founded in 1898 largely because of its proximity to anthracite, the Lehigh Canal and the railroads. Zinc mines were in Franklin, NJ, and an after-thought to many townsfolk.

Signature NJZ buildings are prominent in Palmerton.

In the late 19th century, Stephen Palmer led the New Jersey Zinc Co. to consolidate regional operations here. In 1917, the world's largest smelter opened. Palmerton became a "company town," a model community with well-planned and plentiful housing, educational and cultural opportunities, and good medical care for the residents, who enjoyed the many benefits derived from New Jersey Zinc's social policies.

Today, expansive park facilities, a community pool, a growing library, and Residence Park (the region's most beautiful turn-of the-century neighborhood) continue to make Palmerton an outstanding example of everything a small town should be. Merchants continue to sell hardware, sporting goods, jewelry, groceries and clothing along its wide main street.

Numerous annual events take place in Palmerton. They include a Rolling Cruise in May, Heritage Day in June, and a Community Festival in September. The Lehigh Gap Historical Society has a well-organized, extensive archives af local photos and artifacts at the Borough Hall on Delaware Avenue.

Appalachian Trail hikers know Palmerton as a friendly place to stay over at the Neighborhood House (present day Borough Hall).

The "onion church" was founded by settlers from Austria and Hungary.

Lehigh Gap
Vistas and trails where the river breaks through the mountains

"Lehigh" comes from a Lenni Lenape word meaning "where there are forks."

Over time the Lehigh River carved into the ridges of the Appalachian Mountains, blazing a trail that would eventually become the backbone of future transportation routes. Footpaths along the river banks gave way to canals, then to railroads, and finally to modern-day highways. Nowhere is this more apparent than at Lehigh Gap, a dramatic landscape where the Lehigh River breaks through Blue Mountain, also known as Kittatiny Ridge, the final ridge in the Appalachian chain.

Constriction caused by the mountains means that level land is scarce here, but when you hike up the hillsides and look down, you can easily see all the old transport routes: the river, an abandoned railroad right-of-way, the entrance lock

of the canal, and a highway winding along the Lehigh River. The remnants of industrial pollution has caused unique scarring and mobilized local environmentalists to re-foliate the Gap.

Hikes to try: Three trails will eventually come together here:

1) The Appalachian Trail: The Georgia-to-Maine backpacking trail dips down the northern side of Blue Mountain and crosses Route 248 at a point where river, canal, road, and railroad converge. To access the AT, cross Route 873 as it continues north on the west side of the Lehigh River.

2) The D& L Trail: The railroad right-of-way here runs along the lower edge of

the Lehigh Gap Wildlife Refuge for nearly three miles while paralleling the Lehigh River. Links to other trails are being added. Currently, hiking in this area can be rough due to the uneven railroad ballast surface.

Annual raptor counts are taken along the Kittatiny Ridge.

3) Lehigh & New England (LNE) Trail: A dream and work in progress, this trail follows an old railroad bed 100 feet up the mountain, paralleling the D&L Trail below. The LNE Trail runs 2.5 miles from the Osprey House to the Turnpike Tunnel. You can reach the D&L Trail via the Bob-o-link Trail to create a loop.

Future D&L Trail upgrades also include redevelopment of the former Pfizer Paint Mill property beneath the southern end of the Route 873 bridge. This site will serve as a major trailhead for the all Lehigh Gap area trails.

Lehigh Gap Wildlife Refuge
Birds, critters and a shining example of how land heals

The 800-acre Lehigh Gap Wildlife Refuge near Blue Mountain offers hiking and wildlife observation trails, not to mention beautiful vistas.

The refuge, which can be visited on its own or treated as a stopover during a D&L Trail hike, rests on the Kittatiny Ridge (i.e. Blue Mountain) along the Lehigh River.

Explore the refuge's acreage and you'll wander across wooded slopes, past wetlands, ponds and riparian areas, and through savannahs and grasslands. You'll also encounter a once-degraded area where vegetation was lost to industrial pollutants from a nearby zinc smelter that closed decades ago. Thanks to ongoing restoration efforts, which include strenuous hand-seeding of steep and rocky slopes by volunteer D&L Trail Tenders, the terrain is coming back to life. Eventually, the land will be thick with native, warm-season grasses—a habitat in very short supply in the East—and someday forests, since Trail

Tenders also planted Northern Red Oak acorns along the ridges and trail. The Pennsylvania Audubon Society has declared Kittatinny Ridge an "Important Bird Area," which makes this prime territory for birdwatchers, as well as wildlife photographers.

Hikes to try: The refuge, part of the nonprofit Wildlife Information Center, will be linked to the long-distance Appalachian Trail and offer foot travelers miles and miles of hiking. In the meantime, Lehigh Gap Wildlife Refuge has two good loop trails:

1) Lehigh Gap Loop is the main six-mile hiking path around the refuge. The Osprey Loop is a two-mile hike that begins and ends at the Osprey House.

Parking for the refuge is available at:
• Tannery building and Osprey House
• Junction of Riverview Road and the D&L Trail
• Western end of the LNE Trail
  Continue on Riverview Road to Sunset Road. At the stop sign turn left and then make a quick right. Drive up the hill to the LNE Trail. Parking is on the right.

You can volunteer to help with this restoration project, as well as maintain portions of the D&L Trail by contacting the Delaware & Lehigh National Heritage Corridor "Trail Tenders" program. Email dele.sherry@verizon.net or visit www.delwareandlehigh.org for regular schedule updates.

While not fully operable, Lock #23 is partially restored.

The Locktender's House and Museum at Walnutport.

Simple furnishings exemplify the locktender's family life.

For a pleasant canal town experience and a visual lesson in how canals and locks once functioned, head to Walnutport. Here you'll find Lock #23, which has been partially restored and looks much as it did in the early 1850s.

The Locktender's House was built in 1828 and is one of only two original stone locktender's residences remaining on the Lehigh Canal. The men who lived here with their families were employed by the LC&N to operate and maintain the locks so canal boats could move from one level to the next.

Frank Kelchner was the last locktender to reside in the house. His five children plus hired hands all lived in the small structure—a challenge by today's standards. The locktender earned $200 for a season's work. Schoolboys drove the mules in summer and received two dollars. Canal boats ran from 4 a.m. to 10 p.m., six days a week from April to December.

Today the Locktender's House serves as a museum. You can learn about the town's past as a boat repair

Association, a private, non-profit group that restored and maintains the community's 4.5-mile section of Canal towpath.

Hikes to try: From the Walnutport Locktender's House, you can follow the D&L Trail (towpath) north and view the remnants of Dam #3 at Lehigh Gap. It fed water into the canal at Guard Lock #3, where boats re-entered the canal after a stretch on the Lehigh River. On the hillside just above the active railroad line you'll notice a stone house, which was once the home of the toll collector who collected fees for crossing a chain bridge (ca. 1826-1934) that spanned the river.

One of many quiet spots along the Lehigh Canal.

center and also view a collection of artifacts.

The Walnutport Canal Association has carefully-placed wayside signs and interpretive displays here. There's also a well-maintained community park with plenty of picnic tables.

The third weekend of each October the town hosts the annual Walnutport Canal Festival. It features historical displays, vendors, and residents in period costume from the Canal's glory days. The festival is coordinated by the Walnutport Canal

Then and now: Slate rock is crafted into one of the world's most durable roofing materials.

Slate is a metamorphic rock that starts out as a type of shale and turns hard when exposed to the earth's inner heat. It's the only rock easily split into thin slabs, which accounts for its wide use as roofing on 12th and 13th century castles in England and North Wales.

In 1844 across the Atlantic, in a small settlement along the Lehigh River, someone noticed a slab of slate leaning against a barn owned by resident Peter Heimbach. Thus began Slatington's rise to prominence as one of the world's preeminent suppliers of slate.

Located across from Walnutport on the west side of the Lehigh River, Slatington became the center of the region's Slate Belt. In its heyday, slate was used for everything from durable roofing shingles to chalk boards and pencils in schools. The Lehigh Slate Company's quarries in and around Slatington were among the largest in the U.S., and furnished some of the country's highest quality slate.

A large portion of Slatington's growth and success is directly tied to the opening of the Lehigh Canal, and the ease of shipping that resulted. The town further blossomed when the railroad was built in the late 19th century. Today's traditional downtown with large Victorian homes is a reminder of the commerce generated by the canal, railroad and slate industry. Look carefully and you'll notice elaborate slate roofs that display the beauty of this local building material, which was once shipped as far away as British Columbia to adorn the provincial capital building in that Canadian province. Slatington's streetscape artifacts are closely tied to the story of extraction, processing, transporting, and marketing of slate.

Elaborate Victorian homes are a part of the Slatington National Historic District.

Hikes to try:

Slatington is working to create a D&L trailhead on the site of the former Lehigh Valley Railroad station (just off Main Street after crossing the Lehigh River bridge, where the Lehigh River and Trout Creek converge).

You'll also find a 3.3-mile spur trail known as the Slate Heritage Trail, which meanders along Trout Creek through Slatington and into the villages of Emerald and Slatedale. Along this path, 29 slate quarries once existed. Today only one family-operated quarry is still operating, the Penn Big Bed Slate Quarry in Slatedale. Several slate production sites can be observed along Trout Creek.

From 1880-1930, the Lehigh Valley was the leading slate quarrying center in America. The Lehigh Canal and Lehigh Valley Railroad helped get the product to market.

The first quarry in Slatington was known as the "Tunnel Quarry." Eventually, there were 129 slate quarries between Slatedale and Danielsville.

Roughly 40 percent of slate workers were Welsh. They toiled 11 hours/day during the week, 6 hours on Saturdays, and earned anywhere from $30-$60 a month. At its peak, the local slate industry employed about 2,000 men, boys and girls in the quarries, finishing plants, and transportation network.

Treichlers
Where boats jumped from canal to river

As the Lehigh River makes a winding S-curve at Treichlers, remnants of one of the original "Bear Trap" lock and dam systems can be seen. This lock allowed boats to leave the canal and enter this section of navigable river. A major flood damaged the Three Mile Dam in August 1959. The reconstructed version, which is now breached, measured 500 feet long, 25 feet high and 15 feet deep.

Josiah White designed the Bear Trap lock for the Lehigh.

Coplay
Cement provides strong foundation for a multi-cultural village

Every member of a canaler's family had a job.

To some folks, cement goes unnoticed between bricks and on driveways. But a visit to Coplay will change your perspective on the gray powder that turns rock-hard when mixed with water.

Coplay sits on part of a 400-acre parcel John Jacob Schreiber bought from William Penn's heirs in 1840. The village

time a new furnace was added, so were more homes. As a result, Coplay became a melting pot.

In the spring of 1866, David O. Saylor, Esias Rehrig, and Adam Woolever opened a new business in town. The Coplay Cement Company is located along the west side of the Lehigh River near the Lehigh Valley Railroad. It capitalized on the limestone found in the area.

Ancient Romans invented cement. But it was around 1870 that Saylor revolutionized the

Several of the original Schoefer kilns have been preserved.

was known as Schreibers, until the name Coplay (from "Kolapechka," son of a local Indian chief) stuck to the farming-dominated community of mostly Pennsylvania Dutch and Germans.

Over time, agrarian ways started giving way to industrialization, with the opening of the Lehigh Valley Iron Co. fueling the change. When workers came to the area—a large portion were Irish—the company built houses for them. Each

process. Saylor discovered he could make a cement that hardens underwater from raw materials found in his own quarry. The unique kilns that still stand here and his ingenuity were awarded the first American patent for his particular process of producing high-quality hydraulic cement in 1871. Saylor turned out the first "Portland" cement in 1875, and one year later his brand of cement received a medal at the prestigious Centennial Exhibition in Philadelphia.

Exhibits at Saylor Park commemorate years of safe operations.

Austria, Hungary, Czechoslovakia, Poland and the Ukraine came to work the cement mills. More boarding houses and company buildings arose, and within two decades local villages evolved from disjointed tracts of land bordering cement mills to places where families owned homes and started businesses.

Visit Coplay's Saylor Park to learn more about cement, including the birth and development of the Portland Cement industry. You can also stand at the base of brick ruins that were once massive cement kilns.

Hikes to try: The best way to experience the Saylor Cement kilns is to hike along the Ironton Rail-Trail, a 9-mile path that follows Coplay Creek eastward from North Whitehall to Coplay. The kilns you'll see along the way were taller when built, and were enclosed in a huge building with only the tops exposed.

In Coplay, the separate Ironton section is a 5.5-mile loop that provides quality outdoor recreational opportunities for people of all ages and physical abilities.

The nearby Altas cement plant churned out the cement to build the Panama Canal.

During the first decade of the 20th century the Lehigh Valley became the world's leading producer of Portland cement. Thanks to the high-quality raw materials in the area, Coplay rose to an equally-lofty position of dominance in the American Portland Cement industry, providing cement for concrete used in countless construction projects. Immigrants from

The Ironton Rail-Trail is wide, safe and easily accessible.

The Lehigh Valley was the greatest cement producing region in the world between 1890 and 1940.

In geological lingo, it's known as the Jacksonburg formation and consists of a combination of chalk, clay, shale and limestone. This rock is unique to the Lehigh Valley and is found in a long belt between sedimentary deposits of limestone & shale.

To the folks in Northampton in the late 1800s, it was simply called "cement rock" because it possessed all the necessary ingredients needed to manufacture Portland cement. By using such local ingredients, these hard-working folks were filling 75 percent of the global cement needs by 1900, making Northampton—like its neighbor Coplay—a big reason the Lehigh Valley was the greatest cement-producing region in the world. Earlier, grist mills were adapted to produce hydraulic cement for the canals.

Of all the related industries operating in the "Cement Belt," the most noteworthy was probably the Atlas Cement Plant. Founded in 1895, Atlas provided all the cement used to build the Panama Canal from 1908-1914. The rotary kiln developed there remains the industry standard. The cement was bagged in the Laubach Avenue building that's now the Northampton Area Community Center.

Hikes to try: The Borough of Northampton created a small park along Canal Street, where you'll see that the old towpath has been paved, making a fine walking trail. You'll also find ballfields, picnic pavilions and restrooms.

To access the D&L Trail, leave the towpath and cross the Route 329 bridge. This is the point where the trail switches from towpath to rail-trail and winds along the western side of the Lehigh River. Head north and you'll hit Slatington, Lehigh Gap, and Lehighton. To the south you'll eventually encounter Allentown, Bethlehem and Easton.

Nor-Bath Rail-Trail

Hikes to try: In 1979 Northampton County acquired the rights to an abandoned rail line and created the Northampton-Bath, or Nor-Bath, Rail-Trail. The path, where America's first diesel-powered railroad ran, winds for five miles through scenic, semi-agricultural land in Northampton County between the boroughs of Northampton and Bath. It is open for biking, hiking, bird watching and nature study.

Rail-Trails enrich our communities and countryside.

Currently 3.8 miles of trail are improved with a light-gravel surface. Eventually, the trail may extend for a total of 7.3 miles, pending land use issues.

For more information, contact:
Northampton County Parks and
    Recreation
R.D. 4 - Greystone Building
Nazareth, PA 18064
610-746-1975

Catasauqua
The old furnace was a blast

Catasaqua and the Crane Iron Company were started simultaneously.

In the early 1800s, entrepreneur Erskine Hazard of the LC&N was looking for a new anthracite-burning industry to build along the Lehigh Canal. Hazard enticed Welsh ironmaster David Thomas to the area to develop local furnaces and related industry. Thomas laid out Catasauqua and nearby Hokendaqua, built worker housing, and became prominent in both communities.

By 1845, Biery's Port had a store, church, gristmill, the Iron Works, some homes and two taverns.

Individually, Catasauqua ("dry ground," to local Indians) gained notoriety as the site of the nation's first commercially successful anthracite-burning blast furnace. It began operation in 1839 as the Lehigh Crane Iron Works and was named for George Crane, who had been Thomas' mentor in Wales. The plant's remains are visible today.

Other companies that began in Catasauqua included the Catasauqua Manufacturing Company, the Union Foundry & Machine Company, Davis and Thomas' Foundry, Lehigh Fire-Brick Company, Byden Forged Horseshoe Works, and the Younger Grist Mill.

The George Taylor House, located here, is the 18th century summer residence of the Durham Furnace's talented iron master. Taylor was also a signer of the Declaration of Independence who had four homes on the region. His summer home in Catasauqua is a National Historic Landmark.

Biery's Port Historic District along Mulberry and 2nd streets in Catasauqua is a late 19th -early 20th century urban neighborhood of mixed residential, commercial, and industrial uses. The D&L Trail (towpath here) parallels the Biery's Port district and offers scenic views of Victorian Era homes. You'll also see remnants of Lock #36 at E.L. Schmid, Inc. (formerly Crane Iron Company).

David Thomas opened the Thomas Iron Co. (also known as the Thomas Works) in 1854 at Hokendaqua. In addition to building the furnace plant, the company actually owned the entire town. Hokendaqua's claim to fame was its proximity to the Lehigh Canal and the availability of anthracite for the iron making process.

Hanover Township Canal Park

Many Lehigh Valley towns have trail access.

Located off North Dauphin Street, this Canal Park includes a portion of the D&L towpath, two gazebos, and a pavilion that accommodates large groups. The North Dauphin Street access area has parking, and easy access to both the D&L Trail and Lehigh Canal.

In recent years, the township acquired the nearby Catasauqua Lake property from Lehigh County. This acquisition includes the lake, the existing parking lot, a storage facility on the property, as well as more open space.

This is the final D&L Trail access area before reaching Allentown. From here you can go north to Catasauqua and Northampton along the towpath, continuing on until you jump on the rail-trail at Lehigh Gap. Or head back the other way along the towpath to Bethlehem, Easton and beyond to the Delaware River and its 60-mile length of trail.

Kimmetts Lock

If you need a place to launch your motor boat for some fishing on the Lehigh River, head to this water trail access point located across from the north end of Agere Systems, Inc. (former Lucent Technologies) at North Dauphin and Lloyd Streets, Allentown. Originally built by the Pennsylvania Fish and Boat Commission, this access area is owned and managed by the City of Allentown Parks Department. For more info call 610-437-7628.

Unique partnerships enhance park lands.

Page 105 – Canal boat rides on Josiah White II are available June through October. For more information go to canals.org.

Page 109-110- While agriculture has prevailed in the region up until the present, the rural aesthetic of this area should not mask the industrial vibrancy during most of the nineteenth and early twentieth century.

Page 110- The Bucks County Conference & Visitors Bureau contact information is 3207 Street Road Bensalem, PA 19020 Phone: 215-639-0300 http://visitbuckscounty.com/

Page 111- The D&L Trail is constantly being updated and improved. The "D&L Future Trail" between Morrisville and Bristol is active. For complete and up-to-date information on the trail, please visit: http://www.delawareandlehigh.org/index.php/trail/

Page 119, 122, 127, and 132- The email for Delaware Canal State Park has changed to delawarecanalsp@pa.gov

Page 125- The bridge pictured in the top picture is the Walking Bridge in Lumberville, about fifteen miles downriver from Riegelsville. The D&H Canal in this section refers to the Delaware & Hudson Canal.

Page 131- The phone number for Tohickon Valley Park is 215-297-5625.

Page 138- The canal boat in the picture is a reproduction designed to imitate the original. The New Hope Canal Boat Company is currently closed.

Page 142- The website for Washington Crossing Historic Park is http://www.washingtoncrossingpark.org/

Page 146- The D&R Canal State Park Office contact information has changed. Their new address is 145 Mapleton Road Princeton, NJ 08540 Phone 609-924-5705 http://www.dandrcanal.com/

Page 147- The website for Summerseat in Morrisville is http://historicsummerseat.com/

Page 153- The Bristol Borough's new address is 250 Pond Street Bristol, PA 19007 Phone: 215-788-3828 http://www.bristolborough.com/

Updates to Stone Coal Way
January 2019

Page 10- Delaware & Lehigh National Heritage Corridor address is now 2750 Hugh Moore Park Road, Easton, PA 18042

Page 47 and Page 49- Hickory Run State Park and Lehigh Gorge State park have changed their email to hickoryrunsp@pa.gov

Page 53 and Page 57- The Old Mauch Chunk Landing houses the Jim Thorpe Visitor Center, Lehigh Ave. Jim Thorpe, PA 18229 Phone: 570-325-3673 http://www.delawareandlehigh.org/index.php/visit/old-mauch-chunk-landing-jim-thorpe-visitor-center/

Page 55- The Summit Hill Historical Society is now called the Summit Hill Heritage Center and can be found at 1 West Hazard Street   Summit Hill, PA 18250 Phone: 570-645-7561 http://www.summithillheritagecenter.com/joomla/index.php

Page 57- The Schuylkill County Visitors Bureau's address is Union Station Building 1 Progress Circle, Pottsville, PA 17901 Phone: 570-622-7700 http://www.schuylkill.org/

Page 61- The top picture on the page is of Burgess Lea (The Isaiah Paxson Farm), which is on the National Register of Historic Places. The farm is located five miles above New Hope, and one mile above Center Bridge, in Solebury Township, Bucks County.

Page 61- The lower picture is not of Bethlehem Steel but rather the Lehigh Canal Lock 17 at New Jersey Zinc Co., Palmerton.

Page 62- The Lehigh Valley Convention & Visitors Bureau has become Discover Lehigh Valley. Their new website is www.discoverlehighvalley.com and it includes a complete list of contact information for the visitor centers in the region.

Page 79- To become a Trail Tender volunteer for the Delaware & Lehigh National Heritage Corridor please visit www.delawareandlehigh.org or send an email with your contact information to info@delawareandlehigh.org

Page 88- The Nor-Bath Rail-Trail is currently five miles long. For more information on the trail, contact: Northampton County Department of Public Works   Parks and Recreation Division Phone: 610-746-1975

cont. →

Allentown

Iron, silk, cigars and a busy canal transform
"Allen's Town" into a commerce center

In 1762, William Allen, Chief Justice of Colonial Pennsylvania's Supreme Court, former mayor of Philadelphia and successful businessman, drew up plans for a rural village known as Northamptontown. Folks didn't care for the lengthy, formal name so they called it "Allen's Town."

Allen hoped the location along the Lehigh River would turn his settlement into a thriving business center, but the low water levels made river trade impractical. Sometime in the early 1770s, a discouraged Allen gave the property to his son, James, who built a country home. He called it Trout Hall after his father's hunting and fishing lodge.

Allentown has been nicknamed "Pennsylvania's Park Place."

By the time of the American Revolution, "Allen's Town" was still little more than a small village comprised of Pennsylvania Dutch farmers and tradesmen. In 1829, however, things started to change with the opening of the Lehigh Canal.

The Lehigh Canal helped Allentown become a commerce center.

upstream of the Hamilton Street Bridge. With canal boats loading and unloading goods for Allen's Town, this stretch of river became a major area of commerce.

In 1838 the city officially adopted the name Allentown. In the 1830-40s the Lehigh Valley gave birth to America's industrial revolution. Coupled with the impact of the Lehigh Canal and later the railroads, Allentown finally achieved the commercial success William Allen envisioned.

Canal boats entered the river upstream at Lock No. 39 and exited the Lehigh downstream at the Hamilton Street Dam (Dam No. 7). Many canal workers made their homes on Haymakers Island (later known as Adams Island), located on the east side of the river between today's Hamilton and Tilghman Streets,

Economic growth continued into the 1850-60s with the rise of a strong local iron industry. The nation's growing rail network demanded all the iron Allentown factories could produce. In the years following the Civil War, an

influx of German and Irish workers created an iron-based society along the banks of the Lehigh. Unfortunately, prosperity faded with the collapse of the railroad boom creating the panic of 1873. Big and small iron furnaces closed and sent the local industry into a tail-spin.

The Phoenix Silk Mill was established here in 1881. By the early 20th century, silk mills helped take the place of the iron trade in terms of economics, and Allentown's now-diverse economy produced everything from parlor furniture, and silk, to beer and cigars.

In the 1920s the city commissioned a plan that resulted in Trexler Park. Other parts of an exceptional urban park system include an excellent parkway along the Little Lehigh River.

Since World War II, and most notably since the 1960s, Allentown has undergone another transition. Faced with the decline of manufacturing and the rise of the service economy, the city is once again dealing with change. City officials are currently attracting business to the downtown district, primarily as a way to find new uses for existing structures. A key piece in the puzzle is the proposed Lehigh Landing near the Hamilton Street Bridge. The waterfront redevelopment project would mix transportation, heritage, convention, entertainment attractions, and visitor center.

Allentown's Canal Park is nearby, as well, providing easy access to the D&L Trail, plus opportunities for hiking,

Railroads continue to be an important facet of life in Allentown.

biking, jogging, fishing, and access to the waterways for paddlers.

Allentown Sightseeing

While in the Allentown area, there are a number of places to visit. They include the Liberty Bell Shrine, which marks the spot where the famous symbol of American freedom was housed in 1777. The bell found safe haven in Allentown from the British when it was secreted out of Philadelphia for protection during the struggle for independence. Trout

The Liberty Bell Shrine is at this freedom symbol's exact hiding place.

Hall, the Allen family's colonial stone home has been restored and is available for tours. Also visit the nearby Lehigh Valley Heritage Center. The Allentown Art Museum has fine art collections,

Local Lenapes honor their ancestors along the Little Lehigh.

including paintings and sculptures by Gothic, Renaissance and Baroque masters, as well a Frank Lloyd Wright room installation. The Lehigh Valley Covered Bridge Tour winds through seven bridges, and past the Trexler-Lehigh County Game Preserve. The Museum of Indian Culture honors the native Lenni Lenape people and sits next to the Little Lehigh River, which is a tributary of the Lehigh that flows into the

Delaware River. There are nature trails here, and a section of river that is popular with fly-fishermen. Finally, the Hamilton Street Dam, No. 7 was originally constructed of stone and wood cribbing and stood eight feet high. It was breached in 1979 and replaced by the concrete structure you see today. The present dam has a pool above it for boating and supplies water to the canal below as the old dam did. The Lehigh River's first fish ladder is located here. One of three on the Lehigh, this passageway allows fish such as the American Shad to return to their spawning areas upstream.

Surprising beauty is found in an urban setting.

Lehigh Canal Park
Herons, muskrats and a wildland oasis on the edge of the city

In Allentown, one of the best and easiest ways to access the D&L Trail is at Canal Park, just south of the Hamilton Street Dam between the Lehigh Canal and River. The towpath trail runs through the park and can carry you northward toward Catasauqua, or east toward Bethlehem, Easton and the confluence of the Lehigh and Delaware Rivers. It's about 2.5 miles from the Hamilton Street Dam to the Allentown city limits, and 4 miles to Sand Island (Bethlehem) at the next trail access point. The towpath is well maintained, with a crushed-stone surface. Be alert for wildlife. You may see deer, heron, and turtles along the trail. Please be courteous to others and always use appropriate trail etiquette.

Even though this stretch of the Lehigh flows through Allentown's industrial side, fishermen, canoeists and kayakers frequent Canal Park. Once you're on the river and canal, the scenery and wildlife help you forget you're in a city. It's not unusual to spot a great blue heron, osprey, red-tailed hawk or American kestrel. Muskrats, beaver, woodchucks, wild turkeys, and a variety of ducks and other wildlife inhabit the river bank.

Canal Park is owned by the City of Allentown but the Wildlands Conservancy of Emmaus runs the recreational and educational Bike and Boat Program from its boathouse. One great way to see the landscape is to sign up for a guided canoe trip and paddle to Bethlehem, then loop back on a mountain bike along the D&L Trail. Equipment and safety personnel are included in the cost of a trip.

Also available are two picnic areas located across the footbridge. There are hiking and nature trails, non-motorized biking areas, and a boat launch for both non-motorized and motorized boats. For more information call 610-437-7628.

Bethlehem

Moravian village grows into home of a mighty steel giant

William Penn invited settlers seeking religious tolerance to Pennsylvania. In the mid-1700s, a group of Moravians relocated from North Carolina and settled at the confluence of the Lehigh River and Monocacy Creek. Named on Christmas Eve 1741, their settlement was christened Bethlehem and would become the Lehigh Valley's oldest city. The Moravian ethic supporting high quality industry endured for centuries. Their imprint can still be seen in the downtown's brick and stone buildings.

While the Moravians constructed some water-powered mills on the Monocacy, it was the canal, railroads and resulting economic opportunities that lured large-scale industry to the south bank of the Lehigh River. The largest, Bethlehem Iron Co., soon dominated the economy, town and way of life. Its plants stretched for four miles along the south bank of the Lehigh, and became one of the most striking monuments to America's industrial might. Steel made from local iron, coal and limestone was milled and forged into the many shapes and configurations that helped launch the Industrial Revolution in the late 1800s.

Many of the original structures built by Bethlehem's early settlers still line the streets of the downtown historic district.

Most Bethlehem industries were located along the Monocacy Creek in the 1700s.

The "Christmas City" has six distinct National Historic Districts within its boundaries, as well as two National Historic Landmarks. The Gemeinhaus, built when the missionaries arrived, may be the largest early squared timber structure in continuous use within the United States. The restored 1758 Sun Inn, which once hosted George and Martha Washington, John Adams and Ben Franklin, offers tours and candlelight dining.

"Christmas City" is proud of its historic and cultural resources.

Early history and high quality crafts and trades are the key elements in the Colonial Industrial Quarter on the banks of Monocacy Creek. The Kemerer Museum of Decorative Arts showcases Victorian flair in changing exhibits and restored rooms filled with period furnishings. Turn-of-the-century refinement is evident in the specialty shops and cafes along Bethlehem's Main Street.

Sand Island, located between the Canal and River, is an historic industrial area that has been revitalized as a public City park. It has a river path for paddlers, wood canal dock, tennis and basketball courts, playground, meadow, restrooms and paths for cyclists and hikers. There's a stabilized canal lock here, and the Ice House, making Sand Island a recreational and cultural center for Bethlehem. The Lehigh Canal and towpath run the length of the island.

D&L Trail access: On Sand Island, access for both the D&L Trail and canal is at the east and west ends of the island. Sand Island also has water trail access to the river and canal. At the aqueduct you can access a spur route of the D&L trail that follows Monocacy Creek.

Iron and steel
From ships to skyscrapers, Bethlehem Steel helped build a nation.

Of all the products and businesses born out of the coal-canal connection, none were as significant as iron and a Bethlehem-based industrial titan known locally as "The Steel." Here's a short list of Bethlehem Steel highlights:

1727: First iron furnace opens, on Durham Creek near the Bucks-Northampton County line about 1.5 miles inland from the Delaware River. The furnace produced shot and cannonballs for Colonial and British forces in the French and Indian Wars. Later, it made cannons and ammunition for the Continental Army in the American Revolution. During both conflicts, the furnace was managed by George Taylor, who signed the Declaration of Independence and was a prominent patriot leader.

1840: First successful anthracite-fueled blast furnace in the U.S., created by Welsh ironmaster David Thomas.

1850: After more and more entrepreneurs build anthracite-fueled blast furnaces in the region, the Lehigh Valley becomes America's leading iron producing region, a title it held until 1880. Keys to success included the readily available supply of iron ore, limestone, and coal, plus the canal system that provided easy access to Philadelphia and New York City markets.

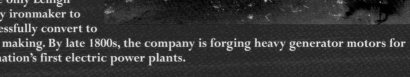

1860: Bethlehem Rolling Mill & Iron Company opens to produce pig iron for wrought-iron rails for railroads. The first rails are produced in 1863.

1873: Bethlehem Iron is the only Lehigh Valley ironmaker to successfully convert to steel making. By late 1800s, the company is forging heavy generator motors for the nation's first electric power plants.

1880-90s: Company builds the first super-heavy forging facility, launching the American defense industry and eventually producing guns, armor plate, propulsion machinery, and nuclear reactor vessels for American and foreign warships. From the end of the Spanish-American War to the beginning of World War I, Bethlehem Iron is the world's largest armaments maker.

Early 20th century: Name changes to Bethlehem Steel. The corporation is run

by Charles M. Schwab, one of industrialist Andrew Carnegie's lieutenants. During his years at the helm, the company starts making structural H beams that are lighter but stronger than anything on the market.

WWI: British government places an order for submarines. The parts are made at the company's shipyard in Fall River, Massachusetts, then shipped to a Canadian yard for assembly. France, Russia, Great Britain, and China order guns and munitions, as well as naval vessels.

1920-30s: Company continues to grow, weathers the Great Depression, and becomes a major erector of bridges and buildings, including: George Washington Bridge over the Hudson, San Francisco's Golden Gate Bridge, Brooklyn Bridge, Gateway Arch in St. Louis, and Madison Square Garden.

1925: Bethlehem Steel retrofits a battle cruiser into the USS Lexington, the nation's first dedicated aircraft carrier.

Pearl Harbor: After the Japanese attack, all phases of Bethlehem Steel shift to war-related production. The shipyards build 1,121 naval and merchant vessels and repair 38,000 ships. The entire company employs 220,000 workers with peak production realized in 1944.

Late 1950s: Company officials increased production capacity 50 percent to meet strong demand for steel during an anticipated growth era. The boom ends in 1958 when the market starts shrinking. The company then faces the longest strike in history (116 days), and the emergence of low-priced foreign steel. Beth Steel continues to upgrade facilities, develop new technology, and diversify.

1990s: Despite best efforts, Beth Steel fades from the industrial scene, closing plants and laying off workers. The Bethlehem facility, once the heart of the mighty industry, closes. Local efforts to preserve key landmarks begin.

The distinctive bullseye was the LC&N logo.

towpath, but the OFA spearheaded efforts to protect the 1829 Locktender's House, mule barn, Lock No. 44, gristmill, and coal yard remnants. They reconstructed the mule barn using canal era tools and equipment and manual labor—part of the reason it took 10 years to complete the project. The multi-functional building now hosts weddings, educational sessions, and interpretative demonstrations.

To see what a difference dedicated volunteers make, head to Freemansburg. Members of the Old Freemansburg Association (OFA) reclaimed their portion of Lehigh Canal from overgrowth and debris, and restored the towpath (D&L Trail).

The Borough of Freemansburg owns a 1.5-mile section of the Lehigh Canal and

Freemansburg is a classic example of a canal town, with houses and other structures built up against the waterway that was the village's lifeblood in the 1800s.

There's limited parking available at the D&L Trail access area off Lockhouse Road near Nancy Run Creek (just off Main Street).

Stone Locktender's House, mule barn and path converge in Freemansburg.

From its headwaters at Gouldsboro, Pa. the Lehigh flows 113 miles until it reaches its confluence with another great river at a place the Lenni Lenape knew as the "Forks of the Delaware." Today, the city of Easton sits on the banks where the Lehigh and Delaware merge. William Penn's son, Thomas, ordered the creation of this new county seat in 1752.

In the early 1800s, construction of the Lehigh Canal and its eventual connection to the Delaware Canal transformed this town into a thriving city. Its riverside location, water power, and steady supply of anthracite helped Easton become an industrial center at a booming crossroads of commerce.

Like other cities designed by Penn, the town's focal point was, and still is, a large "great" square surrounded by

A canaler's life often looked peaceful.

downtown commercial buildings that spread south and east to both rivers. One of three public readings of the Declaration of Independence outside Philadelphia—an act of treason at the time—took place in 1776 in Centre Square. Between 1756 and 1777, Easton was the site of seven Native American treaty councils.

In 1779, Easton became the starting and ending point of General John Sullivan's march against the Iroquois Confederacy.

Lock No. 24 of the Delaware Canal sits on the edge of town overlooking the Forks of the Delaware, where rivers converge, as do the Lehigh, Delaware and Morris canals. Lock 24 offers a close-up view of a canal, and shows how a lock once worked. This spot also

A fully operational lock is located at Hugh Moore Park.

center where kids can create outside the lines (you get to draw on the walls!) and see how crayons are made. Two Rivers Landing and its attractions are located at Northampton & Third Streets, two blocks south of US 22.

The D&L's largest Visitor Center is located in downtown Easton.

Before the American Revolution, thirteen pubs served visitors to Easton, with legal and governmental business conducted therein.

provides a look at a wood and concrete replacement dam. The original stone-and-wood-crib structure marks the lower end of the Lehigh Canal, and supplies water to the Delaware Canal. The original 14-foot-high dam (today's is 25 feet) had an outlet lock so boats could enter the Delaware, then be pulled across the river by cable. Once on the New Jersey side of the river, boats would enter the Morris Canal and make their way to New York Harbor. The Morris Canal entrance portal is still evident on the eastern shore. Look for the stone archway upstream of the railroad bridge.

The best place to begin a journey into Easton's past is Two Rivers Landing. Located on Centre Square in historic downtown Easton, the Landing is home to the D&L Visitor Information Center, National Canal Museum, and the popular Crayola® Factory, an interactive, family-oriented discovery

Centre Square has been a gathering place since the 1700s.

Bachmann Publick House is a living history learning center.

County court sessions, or the Kings Court, were held in local taverns.

The room in the 1753 Bachmann Publick House that served as the Kings Court has been restored to its colonial era appearance. Visitors to the restored tavern can take a step back in time and see re-enacted Colonial and Revolutionary Court proceedings. Located at the northeast corner of Second and Northampton Streets, the Bachmann is Easton's oldest building. It was owned by George Taylor and served as his principal residence.

Walking tours show off many of Easton homes and buildings built by early industrialists. The State Theater, the Lehigh Valley's performing arts showcase, hosts nationally acclaimed stars in concert and theater productions. Horse-drawn carriages rides are also available.

The State Theater—Easton's center for the arts.

Yes, fish can bypass a dam
Especially when they want to breed

It's called a fish passageway, and serves as a shining example of just how far a determined, gilled creature will go to get back to its birthplace, so it can help create the next finned generation. Problems arise when something like a dam gets in the way. And thus, the reason Easton has a bona fide fish passageway, located at Delaware Canal Lock 24.

The passage is actually a series of watery "steps" migrating shad swim through to get past the river's rapids, and struggle upstream to their spawning grounds. This unique display lets you stand below the level of the Lehigh River (underwater, so to speak). During migration you can watch through a window as shad make their way past the dam. Once they bypass the dam, the shad have about 35 miles of river for spawning purposes. Monitoring studies have shown that fish passageways such as the Easton model are part of the reason the Lehigh River's shad population has rebounded in recent years.

Fish passageways aren't a new concept, having been used in England and Ireland since the 1800s. (There are two more upstream.) When dams affect migration and fish must find less suitable spawning habitat, the survival rate of eggs and young fish declines dramatically.

In the Easton area, the D&L Trail consists of 2 sections of towpath, one known as the North Shore Trail on the east side of the Lehigh River—it begins at Hope Road in Bethlehem Township and travels 2.5 miles to the Glendon "Chain" Dam at Riverview Park in Palmer Township. The second section is within the park itself on the west side of the river along the canal.

Hugh Moore Park
Relax, and let the mule do the work

At the edge of Easton you can climb aboard the Josiah White II, a mule-drawn canal boat that will give you a taste of what it was like to slowly wind down the canals back in the 1800s. You'll also find hiking, biking, picnicking, fishing, and canoeing opportunities, all in Hugh Moore Park (named for the wealthy industrialist who invented the paper cup and founded the Dixie Cup Company). Canal boat rides on Josiah White II are available April through September. Call 610-559-6613 for more info. Charters are also available.

Moore was an advocate of parks and open space who endowed his namesake park and the National Canal Museum. His gift enabled the city of Easton to purchase the lower six miles of the Lehigh Canal in 1962. Besides canal boat rides, this park also features a restored Locktender's House and a fully operating section of the Lehigh Canal.

In the middle of the Lehigh River sits Island Park. It once held an amusement park and was connected to Easton by a trolley line that crossed the north channel on a trestle. The island also acted as a canal stepping stone by allowing the transfer of goods from the northern Lehigh Canal side of the river to the opposite New Jersey side and the Morris Canal. The Lehigh Canal towpath (today known as the North Shore Trail) reached the island along a causeway above the island and a mule bridge below. Boats navigated in the pool created behind Dam 8, referred to locally as the Change or Chain Dam. Today, the island is environmentally unique because it contains rare plant species. Paddlers can access the island and view wildlife on either side via the river channels.

Immersion Days—the hands-on way for kids to learn about canal life.

The Chain (Mule) Bridge

In the good old days, after winding down the south shore of Island Park the towpath crossed to the south bank of the Lehigh River along a two-span suspension bridge known as the Chain (Mule) Bridge. Today, masonry abutments and the central pier are in place and in good condition. Still remaining are two early wrought iron suspension cables that held a wooden deck—the towpath, in essence—on which mules and humans could cross the main river channel. The wooden deck (now missing) was supported from the cables by hanger rods. A few remain at the south end.

Below this bridge, the D&L Trail (towpath) continues east along the south bank of the Lehigh River into Hugh Moore Park.

Bridges, canal era remnants, and natural features blend in Easton.

Palmer/Bethlehem Township Bike Trail

Lehigh Valley trails enhance the local quality of life.

lands, residential neighborhoods, and the banks of the Lehigh River. Nearly 30 percent of trail users are commuting to and from work, school, shopping areas, and parks. It links to the D&L Trail at two spots: Hope Road in Bethlehem Township and Riverview Park in Palmer

This 5-mile trail served as one of 10 model rail-trail paths during President Carter's Administration. Today, the eight-foot wide paved trail starts near Easton Area High School and traverses a variety of landscapes, including forests, farm-lands,

Township at the Chain/Change Dam. And despite the name, this "bike trail" is also ideal for walkers, joggers, families and anyone else who enjoys a stroll through the countryside.

FROM EASTON
TO BRISTOL

Centuries-old homes, quaint villages and
tranquil land merge to create the transition
between the Lehigh and Delaware Canals

The Delaware Division
Northampton & Bucks County
A peaceful journey through villages, gentle land and suburbia

Eras and industry converged at Easton to set the stage for fertile Bucks County. The Chain Dam, Guard Lock 8 and the Change Bridge served a bustling warehouse district for farm goods.

From its start at Easton, the Delaware Canal portion of the D&L Trail carries you through land unlike that to the north. The terrain surrounding the southern third of the trail is more expansive. Signs of development dating back to the 1700s that embrace the river, and villages are scattered across a landscape that retains an agrarian flavor.

Events unfolded along the upper Delaware Canal and escaped the heavy industrialism of other areas. The contin-

Even today, rustic agricultural land co-exists with nearby modern industry.

Mule sightings are common in Easton and New Hope.

helped shape pastoral land that offers glimpses of the American Revolution, fieldstone houses, and covered bridges.

This fertile river valley is beloved by artists, past and present, which probably helps explain the air of tranquility and creativity you'll find in many towns. The world here is a surprising mix of a 17th century English manor, 18th century Quaker settlements, 19th century manufacturing, and 20th century development—with a healthy dose of theater, fine dining and the arts thrown in for good measure.

To the south, a pipeline of industrial and commercial activities changed the landscape dramatically. Before suburbanization, truck farming

ued use of canal and river preserved these resources. The success of agriculture and appeal of the land to gentleman farmers helped preserve the rural aesthetic of the region. A free river and the harnessed waters of the Delaware Canal

and sand quarrying were principal occupations. The contrast between the relatively recent industrial landscape and the remaining placid, historic landscapes is striking—contributing to a vibrant economy.

For more information

For info on tours, attractions, seasonal activities, parks, and festivals, please contact the Bucks County Conference & Visitors Bureau, 3207 Street Road, Bensalem, PA 19020. Call: 800-836-BUCKS, or visit: www.bccvb.org

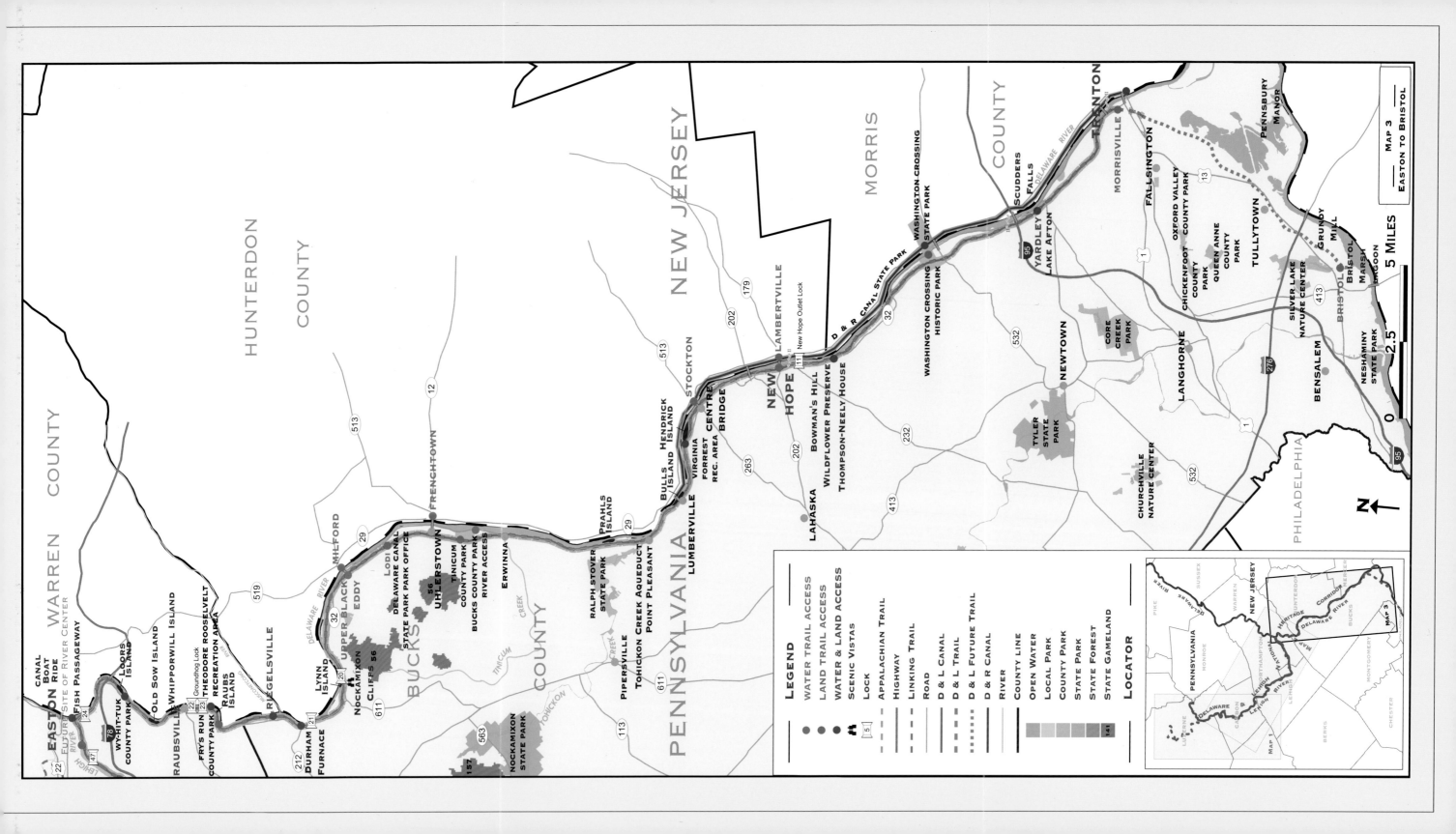

LEGEND

WATER TRAIL ACCESS
LAND TRAIL ACCESS
WATER & LAND ACCESS
SCENIC VISTAS
LOCK
APPALACHIAN TRAIL
HIGHWAY
LINKING TRAIL
ROAD
D & L CANAL
D & L TRAIL
D & L FUTURE TRAIL
D & R CANAL
RIVER
COUNTY LINE
OPEN WATER
LOCAL PARK
COUNTY PARK
STATE PARK
STATE FOREST
STATE GAMELAND

LOCATOR

MAP 3
EASTON TO BRISTOL

0   2.5   5 MILES

N

WARREN COUNTY

EASTON
FUTURE SITE OF RIVER CENTER
CANAL BOAT RIDE
FISH PASSAGEWAY
WY-HIT-TUK COUNTY PARK
LODRS ISLAND
OLD SOW ISLAND
RAUBSVILLE WHIPPORWILL ISLAND
THEODORE ROOSEVELT RECREATION AREA
Groundhog Lock
FRY'S RUN COUNTY PARK
RAUBS ISLAND
RIEGELSVILLE
LYNN ISLAND
DURHAM FURNACE

HUNTERDON COUNTY

FRENCHTOWN
MILFORD
UPPER BLACK EDDY
NOCKAMIXON CLIFFS 56
Delaware Canal
LODI
UHLERSTOWN
State Park Park Office
TINICUM COUNTY PARK
Bucks County Park River Access
ERWINNA
PIPERSVILLE
TOHICKON CREEK AQUEDUCT Point Pleasant
RALPH STOVER STATE PARK
PRAHLS ISLAND
LUMBERVILLE
BULLS HENDRICK ISLAND ISLAND
VIRGINIA FORREST CENTRE REC. AREA
BRIDGE
STOCKTON
NEW HOPE
New Hope Outlet Lock
LAMBERTVILLE
BOWMAN'S HILL WILDFLOWER PRESERVE
THOMPSON-NEELY HOUSE
LAHASKA

BUCKS COUNTY

NOCKAMIXON STATE PARK
NEWTOWN
TYLER STATE PARK
CHURCHVILLE NATURE CENTER
LANGHORNE

PENNSYLVANIA

NEW JERSEY

MORRIS COUNTY

D & R CANAL STATE PARK
WASHINGTON CROSSING STATE PARK
WASHINGTON CROSSING HISTORIC PARK
SCUDDERS FALLS
YARDLEY
Lake Afton
TRENTON
MORRISVILLE
FALLSINGTON
OXFORD VALLEY COUNTY PARK
CHICKENFOOT COUNTY PARK
QUEEN ANNE COUNTY PARK
TULLYTOWN
PENNSBURY MANOR
CORE CREEK PARK
SILVER LAKE NATURE CENTER
GRUNDY MILL
BRISTOL MARSH
BENSALEM
NESHAMINY STATE PARK

PHILADELPHIA

Delaware Canal State Park
A rare park where hiking, biking, and nearby dining and fine art go hand in hand

If there was ever a "living park" this is it. Delaware Canal State Park maintains and protects the 60-mile canal and D&L Trail (or towpath)

You can lace up your lightweight hiking shoes in the morning, shoulder your day pack, start walking, then stop for a lunch of lobster salad, chardonnay and fresh-baked French bread. Or if you prefer, pick out a relatively natural, people-less stretch and enjoy the solitude

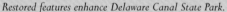

Restored features enhance Delaware Canal State Park.

that follow the course of the Delaware River. Canoeing, hiking, biking, fishing, birdwatching, horseback riding—all your traditional state park-type recreational activities are possible here. But while following the D&L Trail southward through the park, you'll also come upon bustling villages like New Hope, clusters of 150-year-old fieldstone houses, and fertile farmland.

That's what makes this park and portion of trail so fascinating.

over a picnic lunch. You'll find backwoods and small-village life alongside refined amenities.

Scenic bridges, gentle waters and abundant wildlife attract visitors.

< *Please open to Delaware & Lehigh National Heritage Corridor Map 3—Easton to Bristol*

The Recreation Tradition
Recreation on the Delaware Canal is nothing new, and it's still the prime reason people hit the D&L Trail here. Back in the 1800s and early 1900s, folks

Foot, pedal and horse travel: The towpath was used primarily by mules pulling boats along the canal's still waters. Today the D&L Trail/towpath is frequented by joggers, walkers, bicyclists, dayhikers, cross-country skiers, equestrians and birdwatchers. For 30 of its southern-most miles, the trail parallels New Jersey's Delaware & Raritan Canal towpath. Six bridges link the two trails, providing many more miles of recreational opportunities.

Shad, striped bass and trout lure fishermen to the Delaware River.

Boating: Whether you prefer to paddle your craft, or use a motor to skim over the surface of the Delaware River, there are many public access launch areas in both Pennsylvania and New Jersey. (See map for launch areas.) When paddling in the canal (motorboats prohibited), please remember you must portage around the locks.

fished and canoed the canal. When a work scow was available, residents organized boating parties for a ride and picnic. These days, outdoor pursuits generally fall into one of several categories:

Tenting: There are no overnight camp-

Everyday life gets left behind when you paddle downriver.

ing facilities within Delaware Canal State Park, but rental cabins are available in Nockamixon State Park (215-529-7300), and tent camping is allowed in Wy-Hit-Tuk Park and Tinicum County Park. Contact Bucks County Parks at 215-757-0571 or Northampton County Parks at 610-746-1975 for other area camping options.

Environmental Education: The Department of Conservation & Natural Resources has embarked on a new vision for the Park. A first class canal and river recreation and edu-cation program is now available. In the near future a River Center and new offices for the D&L Corridor will be located at the confluence of the Delaware and Lehigh Rivers.

Wildflowers and ferns are plentiful along the Delaware Division.

Trail Etiquette

The Delaware Canal State Park section of the D&L Trail is multi-use, meaning you'll share it with folks whose recreational interests may differ from yours. To make sure everyone gets along, here are some suggestions for proper trail etiquette:

- Always stay on the trail. Delaware Canal State Park is generally no more than 60 feet wide, so don't wander onto private property.
- There is minimal clearance under many canal bridges, so duck and watch your head.
- Keep the canal clean. The park's policy is carry-in, carry-out.

For hikers and runners:
- Stay to the right when on the trail, pass on the left.
- Be courteous and respectful of others, regardless of their speed or skill level.
- Always yield to equestrians.
- Announce yourself when overtaking other trail users.
- When with a dog, obey leash laws. Keep a short leash on your dog when passing other users, and clean up after your dog.

For cyclists:
- Approach and pass others with extreme caution. When approaching from behind, announce yourself well in advance by announcing, "Passing on your left." Reduce speed when passing, and always yield to other trail users.
- Approach blind curves with caution; assume someone is coming in the opposite direction.
- Use appropriate hand signals for turning, stopping, etc.

The whole family can step out and walk along the towpath trail.

- If your approach causes a horse to spook, stop and wait for the rider to tell you it's okay to pass.
- Wear a helmet at all times.

For equestrians:
Equine use is limited because trailer parking is at a premium. Please adhere to the following:
- Make sure your horse has the temperament and training needed for congested trails. This is not the place for training green horses.
- Use common sense; no cantering or galloping on crowded trails.
- Move to the right to allow fast-moving trail users to pass.
- Announce your intention to pass and

reduce speed when doing so. Pass on left.
- Get your horse off the trail if it starts showing behavior problems.
- Use proper hand signals for turning, slowing, etc. and give verbal warnings for dangers on the trail (low branches, holes for example).
- Put a bell on the horse to notify people of your presence.
- Other trail users may not be familiar with horses or how they react. You are an ambassador for the entire equestrian community, so your actions and reactions will reflect on that entire community. Be courteous and answer questions.

Delaware Canal State Park
11 Lodi Hill Road
Upper Black Eddy, PA 18972
610-982-5560
delawarecanalsp@state.pa.us
www.dcnr.state.pa.us

A Canal's Best Friend
Volunteers help keep Delaware Canal watered and working.

An independent, non-profit organization known as Friends of the Delaware Canal (FODC) formed to assist Delaware Canal State Park maintain and improve its facilities. FODC quietly goes about restoring, preserving and improving the canal and its surroundings. Their bottom line is simple: keep water in the canal.

The group accomplishes its goal through advocacy, educational and recreational programs, volunteerism and old fashion fund raising. Among other activities, the Friends sponsor walking and biking events to encourage public use of the canal, schedule clean-ups, and run the Canal Tenders program in which residents monitor sections of the waterway.

D&L Trail Tenders host annual *Share the Trail Day* events to educate users on safe and responsible trail etiquette. These clinics demonstrate how hikers, bikers, and equestrians can mingle on the trail while respecting each other. It's the duty of users and nearby landowners to be good trail stewards and to be respectful of each other!

FODC Membership is available from $25 for individuals, to $500 for "canal superintendent" status. Contact:
Friends of the Delaware Canal
Locktender's House
145 South Main Street
New Hope, PA 18938
215-862-2021
www.fodc.org

Bucks County history
Quaker settlers and an infamous "walking" swindle of Indian land

Bucks County's earliest settlers were English Quakers enticed here by William Penn in the late 1600s. They were attracted to the fertile soil, and

built self-sufficient manor farms and small market villages such as Newtown and Fallsington. These farming communities soon became the breadbasket for Philadelphia, located about 20 miles to the south. Later, Scots-Irish and Germans settled to the north.

Penn got along well with the native Lenni Lenape, but his sons strained the relationship. To relieve debt, they started selling off Indian land west of the Delaware River. When the Lenape disliked the price offered, a solution was proposed: the white newcomers could have as much land as a man could walk in a day.

Instead of walking, the English sent not just a single man but a team of swift runners from Wrightstown to a point near Hickory Run State Park, just north of Jim Thorpe. In the end, the parcel they claimed was roughly 1,200 square miles, or the size of Rhode Island. The Walking Purchase, as the deal became known, frustrated the Lenape.

Nonetheless, the Lenape felt honor bound to fulfill their agreement, and so began their gradual move westward. Each time they settled and were promised by the government that the land would be their permanent home; each time they were eventually forced to relocate. They finally settled 130 years later in Oklahoma and Canada.

The road to everywhere

Whether you plan to hike, paddle, shop or simply enjoy the countryside, you'll take the state-designated Delaware River Scenic Drive. Also known as River Road —it parallels the river and canal—this winding, narrow, two-lane scenic byway is the region's vehicular backbone. Side roads shoot off here and there from this main thoroughfare. The Scenic Drive begins as Route 611 in Easton, then at Kintnersville follows Rt. 32 to Morrisville.

Wy-Hit-Tuk County Park

This small park offers a great view of the canal from the footbridge, a fine nature trail, and picnic pavilion and good access to both the for easy canoe put-ins. No launch permits are needed. Campsites have a backwoods feel. In warm months the leafy foliage provides a sense of privacy, although well-traveled Rt. 611 is just up the hill. Call Northampton County parks at 610-746-1975 for a picnic pavilion permit and camping permits.

Smaller county parks are perfect for first time adventures.

Fry's Run County Park

Quiet waters where small industry once churned.

A lumber operation, tannery and gristmills once thrived here. The reason was free-flowing Fry's Run, which is now a good stream for fly fishermen in search of wild brown trout. Park in the designated lot, then carefully cross Rt. 611 to access Delaware Canal State Park and the trail. Within Fry's Run you'll also find picnic tables and nature trails.

Delaware River Islands Natural Area

River gives birth to sanctuaries for paddlers and migrating birds

Pennsylvania's Bureau of State Parks sets aside Natural Areas to preserve the land's unique scenic, geological, or ecological value. These special places survive and

The Delaware is the longest free-flowing river in the eastern U. S.

thrive as nature intended: without human intervention.

Delaware Canal State Park has two natural areas, both containing threatened or endangered species. One is Nockamixon Cliffs. The other is the River Islands Natural Area, which consists of 11 state-protected pieces of land surrounded by the Delaware River. The river is an important corridor for migrating birds, so these islands make ideal stopover points. They're also good sites for fishermen and canoeists who treat the land with care, and leave no signs of their passing.

Islands, such as Hendricks Island, were once part of the main river shoreline,

but most grew out of the river. The other islands are Loors, Old Sow, Whippoorwill, Raubs, and Lynn Island. Silt and sandstone left behind by glacial waters almost 10,000 years ago form the base of the islands. Seeds deposited by wind, water and wildlife have sprouted, and the growing plants' roots bind the soil together. Although relatively stable, the size, shape and location of the islands shift slightly with the river currents.

Hendricks, locally known as "Island Farm," once held a saw mill, a 112-acre farm and farm house. The main island was designated a Special Management Area due to its archaeological significance. A flood caused by Hurricane Diane in 1955 ruined the few buildings on the island. PECO Energy donated the island to the Bucks County-based Heritage Conservancy, who then turned it over to Delaware Canal State Park.

Delaware River Islands Natural Area
c/o Delaware Canal State Park
11 Lodi Hill Road
Upper Black Eddy, PA 18972
610-982-5560
delawarecanalsp@state.pa.us
www.dcnr.state.pa.us

The Delaware's legendary fish
Shad make a comeback, thanks to cleaner waters.

Of all the fish found in the Delaware River, none are as noteworthy or as popular as the shad. In colonial times, shad were so plentiful and easy to preserve that they became a dietary staple. By 1896, due to abundance and relative ease that they could be caught, millions of pounds had been pulled from the river.

Unfortunately, the increasing growth of cities and industry, dam construction, and pollution caused shad numbers to decline. By 1954 the amount caught dropped to a low of 76,000 pounds.

Thanks to pollution-reduction measures, and ingenious "fish ladders" that help them get up and over dams so they can migrate upstream and spawn, shad are on the rebound. Fish averaging 24-30 inches long and weighing up to 10 pounds have been hooked on the Delaware River in recent years.

Shad live in the Atlantic Ocean and return to their cool, freshwater spawning grounds in the Pocono and Catskill mountains April through July. Young fry hatch in summer and in fall return to the sea, where they remain for three to four years before the spawning urge takes over. Although usually uninterested in eating while making the run upstream, some will strike at lures. For license regulations and general info contact Pennsylvania Fish and Boat Commission at 717-657-4518. Before wetting a hook, check on fishing seasons and permits needed.

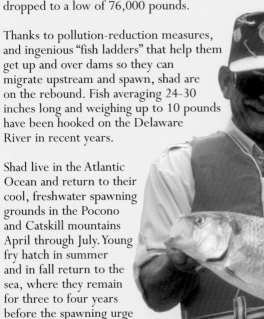

Raubsville

Travellers, including George Washington and Ernest Hemingway have stopped in Raubsville.

The LC&N made many improvements to the Delaware Canal to help it operate more efficiently. LC&N rebuilt and widened several locks, for instance. During the course of all this work, Locks No. 22 and 23 at Raubsville were consolidated into the present Ground Hog Lock. This lock, with a lift height of 17.3 feet was the highest along the entire Delaware Canal. You'll also find restrooms here.

Theodore Roosevelt Recreation and Conservation Area

Locks No. 22 and 23 and a Locktender's House are located here. Restrooms, drinking water, walking paths, picnic tables and grills are available. This is also the site of an old powerhouse for a long-gone trolley.

For paddlers in the canal, there are wooden ramps for easy canoe put-in and take-out. You can't paddle all the way from Wy-Hit-Tuk Park to here because there's a stop gate in the way. Be ready to

There's no shortage of bucolic sights along the Delaware Canal.

carry your canoe as you portage around the lock and put-in just below it at the wooden ramp.

Riegelsville

The village of Riegelsville, a National Historic District, has a fine collection of commercial and residential buildings. Especially impressive are the mansions built by local industrialists.

The bridge over the Delaware River here is one of the few remaining multi-span, highway suspension bridges with continuous cables. For comparison sake, consider that the San Francisco-Oakland Bay Bridge has two large back-to-back suspension bridges, but the cables aren't continuous between the spans.

The existing bridge was built in 1904, as a replacement for the original wooden covered bridge. It pulls on anchors attached to each riverbank and was designed by John A. Roebling & Sons of Trenton, New Jersey. The Roeblings designed the Brooklyn Bridge and the Lackawaxan Aqueduct where the D&H Canal crossed the Delaware River between Pennsylvania and New York. They also provided wire for the suspen-

Historic suspension bridges link New Jersey and Pennsylvania.

sion cables on the Golden Gate Bridge. For paddlers, Riegelsville has a put-in for easy river access (at River mile 174, above Cooks Creek).

Durham Furnace and Lock #21

Interpretive wayside signs describe the workings of the Delaware Canal and life along the waterway.

The original 1727 Durham Furnace was located inland. It produced crude pig and bar iron, as well as cast iron pans, utensils and stove plates for nearly 70 years. Pig iron was the direct product of the blast furnace. When refined, pig iron produced wrought iron. The second Furnace, located closer to the Canal operated from 1848-1908. Today, you'll find a put-in for canoes at the canal but no restroom facilities at this site.

Nockamixon Cliffs Natural Area
A haven for birds of prey and adventurers

As you travel south along the Rt. 611 portion of the Delaware River Scenic Drive, just past Kintnersville you can't help but notice the sheer cliffs towering 300 feet above the river. These are the Nockamixon Cliffs, unspoiled vertical terrain that's perfect habitat for rare plant life, birds of prey and rock climbers.

The process that created the cliffs started back when the only people climbing rocks were those trying to avoid being eaten.

Topography, geology and scenic beauty combine at Nockamixon.

Torrential streams washed massive amounts of reddish sand and mud from the northwest, depositing the sediments into temporary, shallow lakes. The result-

ing red sandstone and shale can still be found throughout the region; it's bright red and easily breaks into flakes and fragments. Toward the end of the Triassic

Spectacular views and ice climbing on the Cliffs.

Period, molten magma from deep within the earth's crust flowed into these beds of sedimentary rock. The "igneous intrusions" heated the surrounding sandstone and shale, changing them into tough, weather-resistant rock called hornfel.

During the Jurassic Period, the region was subjected to continuous erosion. While some rock like sandstone and shale wore away, the hornfel resisted, leaving the Nockamixon Cliffs for us to enjoy today. Because they face north, the cliffs receive little direct sunlight. The resulting cool conditions support an alpine-arctic plant community that's unusual this far south. Just across the Delaware River, opposite conditions occur and create habitat for arid plants.

Nockamixon Cliffs (a Natural Area separate from Nockamixon State Park, which is farther west) were once the site of peregrine falcon nests. The last nests were detected in the 1950s. However, each spring red-tailed hawks and osprey circle above.

You're welcome to explore this State Natural Area, but are asked to abide by the "take only pictures, leave only footprints" policy. Camping is prohibited.

Nockamixon Cliffs Natural Area
c/o Delaware Canal State Park
11 Lodi Hill Road
Upper Black Eddy, PA 18972
610-982-5560
delawarecanalsp@state.pa.us
www.dcnr.state.pa.us

Upper Black Eddy

Paddlers should use caution at this Pennsylvania Fish and Boat Commission launch site. Larger boats are common, as are low-water conditions.

River running and water trails: Fun for families and "rats"

Whether you're a novice wanting to get your feet wet for the first time or a veteran river runner (a.k.a. "river rat"), the Delaware River will suit your needs.

Most of the Delaware through central Bucks County is Class I, which means it's suitable for tubing and family canoeing. The exception is the Class II-III whitewater rapids at Lambertville Wing Dam (Wells Falls) just below New Hope, and at Scudders Falls north of Yardley. In fact, you cannot canoe beyond the wing dam near Lock. No. 8 just below Lambertville. Tohickon Creek in Bucks County offers solid Class III+ whitewater (advanced river rats only) from Ralph Stover State Park to Point Pleasant, PA—about 15 miles.

The 65-mile portion of the Delaware River from Delaware Water Gap to Washington Crossing Historic Park is included in the National Wild and Scenic Rivers program. For Delaware River Water Trail access info, a recreational guide/map is available from:

Delaware River Basin
    Commission
25 State Police Drive
P.O. Box 7360
West Trenton, NJ
    08628-0360
Phone: 609-883-9500
Fax: 609-883-9522
http://www.state.nj.us/drbc/

Lodi Lock #19: Park Headquarters

Visitor information is available at Park Headquarters in Lodi.

The name "Lodi" either comes from a variety of locally grown summer apple or for a village in Italy. But it's also the name of the settlement where Delaware Canal State Park headquarters are located. Here you can ask any and all questions, and pick up plenty of printed materials for a more informed, enjoyable adventure. Turn off Rt. 32 onto Lodi Hill Road to reach the office. Look for the signs.

Tinicum County Park

Located near the town of Erwinna along Rt. 32, Tinicum Park boasts 126 acres and is the site of the Erwin-Stover House, an 1800s Federal-style home.

The Delaware River and Canal separate a bit at Tinicum, with the river on one side of Rt. 32 and the canal across the road

The polo season at Tinicum runs mid-May through early October.

behind a cluster of houses. Along the river is Stover Mill, a 19th century structure that's been turned into an art gallery that still houses some of the original mill equipment.

The park has playgrounds, picnicking, hiking, ball fields, boating, fishing, camping, and restrooms. On Saturdays during the summer and early fall, you can observe a polo match.

"High Rocks" offers a scenic vista of a horseshoe bend.

This 612-acre park, named for Tohickon Creek, is known to be one of the cleanest in the state. It has the second largest stream in Bucks County (behind Neshaminy Creek). Large dams and gristmills were once scattered along its banks. Today, only the Stover-Myers Mill remains, and a pair of covered bridges span the creek on the E. Rockhill-Haycock line. Tohickon Creek is currently classified as a cold water fishery and is stocked with trout each year.

For great views, head to the area known as High Rocks. It is located on Tory Road a short distance from the park. This sce-nic overlook of Tohickon Creek sits atop 200-foot, sheer, vertical cliffs of red Brunswick shale that attract rock climbers from near and far. Trails on either side of High Rocks lead to either Tohickon Valley County Park or the adjoining Ralph Stover State Park. Most of the park's trails are excellent for mountain biking and hiking, and follow old logging roads through stands of oak, hickory, tulip popular, hemlock and white pine. Usually the straightest and tallest trees in the forest, tulip poplars are also subtly colorful with greenish-orange flowers that bloom in mid- to late-spring.

Tohickon (Lenape for "Deer Bone Creek") Valley Park, High Rocks, Stover-Myers Mill and the Tohickon Creek are a photographer and birdwatcher's paradise. Bucks County Audubon Society surveys show that the creek valley houses 82 bird species, including four of rare concern and 10 rare breeders. In the fields and meadows you'll find bluebirds nesting in the spring, and the woodlands are home to pileated woodpeckers. Hawks, owls, and woodcocks are also common.

In the late spring, the scent of wildflowers fills the air and reminds you of areas farther north where the mountains house a variety of fragrant flora. The forest is mostly hardwoods. *Warning: Copperheads are poisonous. Although not known to be aggressive,*

The restored Tohickon Aqueduct (ca. 1832) allows water to flow into the Point Pleasant section of the Delaware Canal.

they can be found in and around rock piles along Tohickon Creek.

Available cabins and campgrounds are busy during the well-known water releases in late March and early November. For two days water flows from Lake Nockamixon at a rate of 500 cubic feet per second, turning the usually-quiet Tohickon Creek into raging Class III and IV whitewater. The best rapids—for running, or for sitting and watching others brave the churning water—are around cabin 4.

The park is open year-round.
Tohickon Valley Park
c/o Bucks County Parks & Recreation
Cafferty Road
Point Pleasant, PA
215-757-0571 ext. 3301

Photo opportunities abound.

Ralph Stover State Park

Great fishing, with views courtesy of author
James Michener

Hiking at Ralph Stover provides striking views of cliffs and the millrace.

Ralph Stover Park borders Tohickon Creek and was the site of a late 18th century, water-powered grain mill; some of its remnants are still clearly visible. The High Rocks Scenic Vista, a gift from author James A. Michener a few years after the park opened in 1935, offers outstanding long-distance views of the creek, its oxbow, and the surrounding forests.

Both adventurous and gentle recreational opportunities can be found at this 45-acre park. Each March and November, planned water releases from Lake Nockamixon turn Tohickon Creek into a challenging course for canoers and kayakers. The creek contains several drop-offs, especially downstream of the High Rocks cliffs, so paddlers should exercise caution.

If fishing is your game, you'll find warm-water species like smallmouth bass, sunfish, carp and catfish in Tohickon Creek. The Pennsylvania Fish and Boat Commission stocks trout (cold-water species only). State fishing regulations apply.

Hikers will find a 1-mile trail. For picnicking, there's a shaded area with drinking water, tables, pavilions, fireplaces and restrooms.

Ralph Stover State Park
c/o Delaware Canal State Park
11 Lodi Hill Road
Upper Black Eddy, PA 18972
610-982-5560
delawarecanalsp@state.pa.us
www.dcnr.state.pa.us

State Park Regulations

Be prepared. Bring proper equipment.
You are responsible for you and your group's safety.
Alcoholic beverages are prohibited.
Pets must be leashed or restrained.
Enjoy wildlife from safe distance and do not feed.
Build fires only in designated facilities, and properly dispose of coals.
Do not leave your fire unattended.
Park only in designated areas and obey all traffic regulations.
Please recycle. Place trash in proper receptacles, or take it home with you.

What's that in the sky?
Suggestions and tips for friends of the feather

The Delaware River region offers some of the best birdwatching to be found along the D&L Trail. Here are some feathery tidbits:

• Paddle the river or hike the D&L Trail and you may see: mallard and black ducks, turkey vultures, sparrows, marsh hawks, ruffed grouse, owls, downy woodpeckers, chickadees, Carolina wrens, starlings, song sparrows, robins, cardinals, goldfinches, whippoorwills, Canada geese. Closer to the coast: seagulls, egrets, herons and osprey.

• While there's been a drastic decline of ring-neck pheasants in the Delaware Valley, there has been an increase in wild turkeys and a population explosion of house finches.

• The lower end of the D&L Trail is within the Atlantic Flyway, one of the four major waterfowl migration routes in the U.S.

• Bald eagles are common along the Delaware River. Look for nesting sites along the shoreline and on islands.

• Ospreys are migratory, arriving March-May and leaving Sept-Nov. They nest in dead snags, living trees, channel bouys, chimneys, utility poles, and windmills. Because their diet is almost always fish, osprey usually nest above or near water. They often return to the same nesting site year after year.

Hardwood Heaven

"Pennsylvania" is Latin for "Penn's Wood," so it's no wonder hardwood trees are so plentiful here. The D&L Trail's Delaware section has a variety of impressive broad-leafed trees that'll have you craning your neck in awe and checking your field guide to identify each species.

The most common trees include giant sycamore, tulip poplar, oak, locust and willow. You'll also find hickory, beech, red maple, white ash, cherry, black walnut, and elm. Fall is prime time for these hardwoods, when their leaves turn orange, red and golden and attract a car-based species of gawking humans known as "Leaf Peepers."

Hemlocks are found in ravines and on damp northern slopes. Dogwoods grace the hillsides and are especially pleasing to the eye during the spring bloom. Red cedar are common in Bucks County.

Just don't walk around too long with your eyes skyward. Bump into too many tree trunks and you'll go home with a serious case of bark nose.

Virginia Forrest Recreation Area

This area is named for the conservationist who was instrumental in having the Delaware Canal designated a National Historic Landmark. Parking, restrooms, river put-ins for paddling, potable water, the towpath trail and picnic tables are all to be found at this site.

TOWPATH TRAIL: Refers to sections of the D&L Trail that wind through Delaware Canal State Park and along the Lehigh Canal from Easton north to Jim Thorpe. These paths were once used by mules towing canal boats. From White Haven north to Wilkes-Barre, the trail follows abandoned railroad bed.

GREAT RIVER: Name the native Lenni Lenape gave to the Delaware River.

5 FEET: Average depth of Delaware Canal while it was in commercial operation.

4 A.M. – 10 P.M.: Canal workers' hours. A typical day started with grooming and harnessing the mules, and ended when locktenders called it a day.

33 MILLION: Tons of anthracite coal shipped on the Delaware Canal's waters during its lifetime.

HALF CENT PER TON, PER MILE: Typical charge for using the Delaware Canal. The standard canal boat was 87 feet long, 10.5 feet wide, and held about 80 tons of cargo—usually coal, lumber, limestone, iron or produce.

165 FEET: Distance, in elevation, the Delaware Canal drops over its 60-mile length.

23: Total number of lift locks within the Delaware Canal.

10: Number of aqueducts where the Delaware Canal flows over a small valley or stream.

2 WORK DAYS: Time it took a loaded boat to make the Easton-to-Bristol run. Mule teams may have been changed three to four times along the way.

CANVASS WHITE: Chief engineer on the Delaware & Raritan Canal, who also served as an engineer on the Erie and Lehigh canal projects. His work crews used picks, shovels, wheelbarrows, and horses. White also developed and patented an early formula for hydraulic cement.

EAST COAST GREENWAY: An audacious project to create a 2,600-mile multi-use path linking East Coast cities from Maine to Florida. This route would include a part of the D&L Trail and serve as an urban alternative to the popular Appalachian Trail used by hikers and backpackers.

CONCH SHELL: Used as a sounding horn to signal the arrival of a canal boat at a lock.

New Hope

River town evolves into a magnet that lures arts and theater aficionados

Scenes along the Delaware Canal towpath have long delighted the eye.

It's easy to use the word "bustling" to describe New Hope, since the village is so alive with galleries, specialty shops, both casual and fine dining, and theater. People travel from Philadelphia, New York City and beyond to spend the day shopping and dining at what started out as an early industrial town.

New Hope was bustling back in the late 1700s, too. By one 1798 account, there are "34 buildings and dwellings," including "stores, shops, barns, a tavern, stables and saw mills"—a veritable metropolis, compared to other settlements up and down the Lehigh and Delaware rivers. The town boasted a variety of mills, ranging from the usual grist and lumber, to those that produced flour and processed flax (rendering flaxseed oil, and twine made from flax and hemp). In

Interesting niches are numerous.

New Hope: simultaneously quaint and curious.

stone house once owned by Major Edward Randolph, a patriot of 1776.

Along Main Street you'll find a handsome stone mansion built by noted civic leader Benjamin Parry. It took three years to complete, and today the 1784 Parry Mansion stands as a fine example of 18th century architecture. The house is open for tours that highlight 125 years of decorative changes from 1775-1900.

Parry also had a hand in building the first bridge that linked New Hope with Lambertville across the river in New Jersey. Along with businessman Samuel Ingham, Parry in 1812 received legislative permission to construct a covered wooden bridge with six spans. The project took two years to complete, and in the end the cost of constructing the bridge and toll booths, plus purchasing ferry rights totaled $48,000—a king's ransom back then. A portion of the bridge was

the 1820s, cotton spinning and weaving joined the list of local businesses when facilities opened on the banks of the Delaware.

Veterans from the American Revolution and War of 1812 have called New Hope home, and the streets are lined with houses dating back to that era. Most of the oldest houses are on Ferry Street. On the south side of the street is an old

Residents and businesses take great pride in their properties.

Mules tow passengers in authentic canal boats at New Hope and Easton.

destroyed by a flood in 1841. In 1903, the New Hope side of the old wooden bridge was so damaged by another flood that it was replaced by an iron structure.

As was the case elsewhere along its route, the canal brought life and energy to New Hope. In 1882 one resident wrote in a letter that "a great deal of coal is coming down." By some accounts, in the late 1860s an estimated 100 canal boats a day passed through New Hope.

During the 1920s and 30s, the village, nearby hamlets and farms became a flourishing art colony. By the mid 1900s New Hope was a popular resort, a stopping point for plays bound for Broadway, and home to New York and Philadelphia artists, musicians, and writers. So many artists have worked in and around the town that the New Hope School of Pennsylvania Impressionists was born. Today, the theater and art scene help draw more than a million sightseers a year, many choosing to ride the mule-drawn canal boat (more info below) and

refurbished New Hope & Ivyland Railroad, with its steam locomotive and antique coaches. Displays at the 19th century Locktender's House, located at Lock No. 11, depict canal workers and their families at work and play.

One- to three-hour mule-drawn canal boat trips are available, weekends in April, daily May through October.

New Hope Canal Boat Co.
149 South Main Street
New Hope, PA 18938
215-862-0758
www.canalboats.com

Casual charm along the canal.

Durham boats
The locally made, pre-canal vessels of choice

In the days before the Delaware Canal opened, some shipping needs were handled by Durham boats, which were originally built in the town of Durham located upriver near Riegelsville. The boats were propelled downstream by the current and oars. A long steering oar and setting poles took them upstream. They were up to 40 feet in length and usually manned by five men, who managed to safely navigate the river's shoals, islands and rapids far better than larger ships could. Until the canal was complete in the early 1830s, Durham boats carried flour, grain, whiskey and other supplies needed throughout the Delaware Valley farming region. They were also the vessels of choice for George Washington and his men when they made their victorious Christmas 1776 crossing of the Delaware River.

Bowman's Hill Wildflower Preserve
The way land is supposed to be: natural and lush with wildflowers

Wildflowers, birds and wildlife are among the pleasures found along Route 32.

Visit Bowman's Hill Wildflower Preserve and you'll know how your average bee feels when first encountering the place: with so many wildflowers, you won't know where to start.

The preserve is 100 acres large and thick with more than 1,000 species of native trees, shrubs, vines, wildflowers and ferns, all in a natural, wooded setting. But besides the natural beauty, this is also a place of learning. The two dozen well-marked interpretive trails, many following Pidcock Creek at the base of Bowman's Hill, feature labeled plaques that

A 110' stone watchtower has marked the role Bowman's Hill played in the American Revolution.

Association in cooperation with Pennsylvania Historical and Museum Commission, is open year-round. You'll find a Visitor and Resource Center with trail maps, bloom guides, plus info on programs and tours. The center also houses the Twinleaf Gift Shop, Sinkler Bird Observatory, Platt Bird Collection, educational exhibits, and restrooms.

If you tire of wildflowers, be sure to check out the Bowman's Hill Tower. Built in 1930 to commemorate this important Revolutionary War lookout site, the tower rises 110 feet above the ground, offering a panoramic view of the countryside.

The Thompson-Neely House, the oldest section of which dates to 1702, was the December 1776 headquarters of patriot general Lord Stirling. The house and nearby outbuildings can be toured, as can the restored Thompson-Neely Grist Mill. There's also

tell you specifically what variety of flora you're admiring.

The preserve was founded in 1934 by legislative act, and is also the official State Wildflower Preserve. Its purpose is to encourage a greater appreciation of native plants, and to foster a commitment of preservation that will insure a healthy, diverse natural world. All you need remember is that this is a great place to be when the bloom is on.

The property, governed by the nonprofit Bowmans Hill Wildflower Preserve

the century-old gristmill that's in such good shape that hopefully it'll be operational in the not-too-distant future. Because of its natural setting, Bowman's Hill also offers great birdwatching.

Open daily 9-5, grounds open 8:30 a.m. to sunset. Closed Thanksgiving, Christmas and New Year's Day.

Bowman's Hill Wildflower Preserve
1635 River Road (Route 32)
New Hope, PA 18938
215-862-2924
www.bhwp.org

In the early morning of Dec. 26, 1776 George Washington and 2,400 Continental Army troops marched into Trenton, N.J., and surprised the Hessian and British forces camped there. For the tired and oft-beaten Continental forces, the resounding victory re-ignited the cause of freedom and gave new life to the American Revolution.

The 500-acre Washington Crossing State Historic Park, located about six miles south of New Hope on River Road, doesn't commemorate the victory per se. Instead it honors an almost-as-noteworthy achievement that occurred Christmas night. Under cover of darkness and in a blinding sleet and snowstorm, his men wearing little more than rags, Washington crossed the frozen Delaware River.

It ranks as one of the boldest moves in military history, and each Christmas at 1 p.m. the event is reenacted; some years, in front of 100,000 visitors. During this annual celebration, you can watch re-enactors in Continental military dress cross the river in replica Durham boats like the ones Washington used.

The Park is divided into two areas. The Thompson-Neely House section is 1.5 miles southeast of New Hope on Route 32, and functioned as an infirmary

Artistic renditions of Washington crossing the icy Delaware are universally recognizable.

during battles and was also a grist mill. The McConkey's Ferry section, 5 miles farther south, is the site of the visitor center. There you'll find a video that tells

A reenactment of Washington Crossing the Delaware occurs each Christmas Day at 1 p.m.

of the 10 days from the time of the crossing through the revolutionaries' victories at Trenton and Princeton.

You'll also see houses and work buildings that represent Pennsylvania industry and home life in the 18th and 19th centuries. The McConkey's Ferry Inn, for instance, served as a guard post during the Continental Army's 1776 encampment in Bucks County.

Several 19th century sites can also be seen, including the 1817 Mahlon K. Taylor House, which has been restored to reflect the lifestyle typical of a success-ful, affluent businessman of the era. The Taylorsville Store, a general store built in 1828, is open to the public, and the 1823 Hibb's House is the site of open-hearth cooking demonstrations. The Blacksmith's House offers occasional spinning and weaving demonstrations. Replicas of the heavy wooden Durham

boats can be seen in the Durham Boat House. Such boats were originally used to haul iron ore. Finally, the graves of America's first unknown soldiers and Captain James Moore (d. December 25, 1776) can be seen at the park.

The small 19th cen-tury village of Taylorsville, located within the park, is clustered around one of the ornate steel bridges that span the Delaware River.

Many of the build-ings are owned by the Pennsylvania Historical and Museum Commission, which also owns 500 surrounding acres.

Individuals or groups can tour all of the historic houses. School groups can request a guided tour. Throughout the year the park presents a wide array of events and programs for the family, including encampments, and demonstra-tions of Colonial chores and crafts. Call for a schedule.

The park and historic buildings are open Tuesday through Saturday, 9 a.m. to 5 p.m., and Sunday Noon until 5 p.m. (closed January 1 and Thanksgiving).

Washington Crossing Historic Park
1112 River Road
Washington Crossing, PA 18977
Phone: 215-493-4076
Hours: Tue-Sat 9 a.m.-5 p.m.;
Sun 12 p.m.-5 p.m.
www.phmc.state.pa.us

Yardley

A quaint, town with a historical feel—despite the big cities down the road

By 1710, Yardley's Ferry was established and later developed into a major river crossing.

Yardley's roots stretch back to 1682, when Englishman William Yardley paid William Penn 10 pounds for 500 acres of land. It wasn't until 1807 that Yardley began to develop into a village, and by 1880 the population stood at 820 residents. Early industries included a spoke and handle factory, sawmill, plate and plaster mill, and two flour mills. The first post office, established in 1828, carried the name "Yardleyville," but the name was shortened to Yardley when the Reading Railroad came through in 1876.

During the Civil War, Yardley was safe haven on the Underground Railroad, an escape route for runaway slaves. Known hiding places were under the eaves of the Continental Hotel (now the Continental

Tavern), in warehouse bins along the Delaware Canal, and at the town's General Store (now Worthington Insurance). At Lakeside, the yellow house facing Lake Afton, one brick-walled cellar room is also thought to have been a hiding place.

Lake Afton is a man-made mill pond you'll find downtown at Main Street and Afton Avenue. The small lake was first noted in a deed dated 1713, and was created to provide water to run the grist mills. These days, it's a popular spot for ducks, fishermen and ice skaters.

Elsewhere in town you'll find the Yardley Grist Mill, which has been a center of commerce since its inception in the late

Yardley preserves the best of its past yet offers convenient suburban living along the Delaware River.

ples of Second Empire, Queen Anne, and Victorian Gothic architecture, all enhanced by the presence of trees and shrubs carefully planted to lend the town a residential, neighborhood feel. The historic district encompasses both sections of Canal Street, which runs parallel to the Delaware Canal and is dotted with small, predominantly frame structures dating from 1840. Along the southernmost section of Canal Street is the small, frame Yardley-Bethel A.M.E. Church built in 1877. Several canal bridges and an aqueduct are within the district, as well.

East of the canal along the south side of East Afton Avenue you'll find rows of stone homes that mirror the street's pre-canal days.

1600s. During the Civil War the mill supplied thousands of tons of sorghum and meal to Union soldiers. By 1926 the mill had ceased operation, and has since been restored and now houses several businesses.

Until the mid-20th century, the surrounding countryside was relatively open farmland. While the past two decades have seen much of the agricultural landscape give way to residential development—the area is a bedroom community for Philadelphia, Princeton, and New York—much of Yardley per se has retained its historic integrity. A large part of that is due to the town's preservationist ethic and the creation of a well-maintained historic district.

The majority of the buildings within the district are along South Main Street, where you'll find exam-

The waters of Lake Afton are a refuge for migrating ducks.

Delaware & Raritan Canal State Park

New Jersey park provides another world of recreational and entertainment possibilities

"Trenton Makes The World Takes" is a glowing welcome mat for all who enter NJ from Morrisville.

Though it's not a part of Delaware Canal State Park, a portion of New Jersey's Delaware and Raritan Canal State Park (the section from Morrisville to Frenchtown) has six river bridge links with the D&L Trail. When combined, both parks' trails offer almost limitless opportunities for hiking, biking, birding, jogging and horseback riding in both Pennsylvania and New Jersey. (See page 146 and map for exact locations of the six D&L/D&R trail links.)

The D&R Canal was completed in 1834, and when combined with the Delaware and Raritan rivers, creates a link between Philadelphia and New York City. The canal's peak years were the 1860-70s

Just across the river from New Hope, Lambertville, NJ is home to countless antique shops.

-145-

when 80 percent of its total cargo was Pennsylvania coal. By the late 1800s, the speed and power of railroads had displaced the canals and the D&R's last profitable year was 1892, although the system remained open until 1932.

The D&R Canal and its various structures were listed in the National Register of Historic Places in 1973. A year later 60 miles of canal and river-side land became a state park. The right-of-way for the old Belvidere-Delaware Railroad was added to the park in the 1980s, and the

D&R's trail system was designated a National Recreation Trail in 1992.

Besides the D&R's cultural and historic significance, the park is also a valuable wildlife corridor. A recent bird survey revealed 160 different species, with almost 90 percent nesting in the park.

D&R Canal State Park Office
625 Canal Road
Somerset, NJ 08873
732-873-3050
www.dandrcanal.com

The Pennsylvania-New Jersey Connections
Bridges let you jump from the D&L Trail to an equally fine path on the other side of the Delaware River.

There are six links between the D&L and D&R trails, all of which will carry you across the Delaware River, back and forth from Pennsylvania to New Jersey. They are marked by descriptive interpretive and directional signs. They include: Uhlerstown, PA to Frenchtown, NJ; Lumberville, PA to Bulls Island, NJ; Centre Bridge, PA to Stockton, NJ; New Hope, PA to Lambertville, NJ; Washington Crossing, PA and NJ; and Morrisville, PA to Trenton, NJ.

The Canal and Suburbia
William Penn builds a mansion, steel yields a commuter community, and the canal rises from a mall's ashes

Stately stone homes and converted farms are interspersed with recent suburban development.

The stretch of trail from Morrisville to Fairless Hills provides an interesting look at how suburbia shapes the land. The Delaware Canal is preserved as green space amidst industrial development and trailer parks. It also offers a lesson in how determination and perseverance can help to reclaim what was once thought lost to development.

Morrisville

Named for Robert Morris, financier of the American Revolution, the town of Morrisville is located at the falls of the Delaware River across from Trenton. Historically, the town has strong ties to both Trenton and Philadelphia.

One-half mile from the Falls of the Delaware River, nobleman Thomas Barclay's 1765 Georgian mansion served as Washington's headquarters Dec 8-14, 1776. Declaration of Independence and Constitution signers Robert Morris and George Clymer were subsequent owners. Summerseat, as this home is known, is a National Historic Landmark. It is located at Hillcrest & Legion Avenues, and is open to individuals and groups. Call 215-295-7339 for info.

As far as the D&L Trail goes, this is where the canal departs from its course paralleling the river and heads to Bristol.

Fallsington

This 300-year-old Quaker village features over 90 buildings from the 18th and 19th centuries. In more recent times steel was king, as evidenced by the remnants of U.S. Steel's enormous Fairless Works. The steel-making complex was built in 1953 on the Delaware River, where water for cooling, wastewater and shipping was readily available. Nearby Levittown, a planned community designed to house factory and mill workers (and now a bedroom community of Philadelphia), helped attract waves of post-war immigrants, some migrating here from the declining coal and manufacturing regions at the northern end of the D&L Trail.

The Fallsington-area landscape dramatically changed in the 20th century. In canal days, before the 1930s when it ceased operation, this region was predominantly agricultural—except for a narrow strip of industrial and commercial activities along the canal itself. But due to its proximity to Philadelphia, Trenton and the eastern metropolitan corridor, the land became too valuable to keep in crops, and quickly turned into suburbia.

Tullytown

After World War II ended, lower Bucks County experienced tremendous economic growth and development. The Delaware Canal south of Morrisville took a back seat to the urbanization, and nowhere was this more evident than in nearby Tullytown. It was here, in the 1950s, that a new type of commercial development—the shopping center— was built along the Levittown Parkway at Route 13. Unfortunately, during construction the canal was diverted into a siphon pipe, filled in and paved over for a parking lot.

The recent closing of the shopping center presents an opportunity to restore the canal and re-connect the towpath. The first phase calls for a pedestrian

New housing development is changing the landscape in Bucks County.

bridge to be built over busy Route 13, linking portions of the towpath that are currently separated by the highway. The bridge is to be located at Tullytown and will resemble the historic suspension bridges that traditionally spanned the Delaware River. This bridge would be a highly-visible, dramatic marker for the Delaware Canal and Trail along Route 13. It would also provide safe highway crossing for D&L Trail users, as well as for visitors to the new Bristol Township Park at nearby Lock #4.

William Penn embraced the beliefs of the Society of Friends.

Phase two plans call for a second pedestrian bridge to be located farther south at the I-95/Pennsylvania Turnpike intersection. Phase three will see re-construction of the towpath at the Levittown Shopping Center, with the final phase consisting of repairing the canal so it can once again hold water.

Pennsbury Manor

The 17th-century, Delaware River country estate of William Penn—statesman, diplomat, and founder of Pennsylvania—is nearby. Penn believed in equality of the races, and that life in the country was more wholesome than the worldly atmosphere of crowded cities. His

The recreation of Penn's Delaware River-front home was built in the late 1930s.

only a 70 x 100 foot lot—ideal for steel workers and blue collar wage earners looking to break into the housing market. The low cost housing was also perfect for a planned community brothers Alfred and William Levitt envisioned on farmland they recently purchased in lower Bucks County.

Ten weeks after their exhibit center opened, 3,500 Levittowners and similar models were ordered. Levitt & Sons construction company would eventually complete about 200 houses a week. Levittown was to be completely self-contained, with schools, places of worship, recreation areas and shopping facilities. The Levitt brothers' plans also included landscaping, and a washing machine, stove and refrigerator in each house. By signing an agreement of sale, each owner pledged not to erect a fence, change the color of their house, or hang laundry out on Sundays. When laundry was hung out, only umbrella-type clothes-lines were permitted.

Today, more than 50 years later, Levittown is eligible for listing on the National Register of Historic Places, and plans are underway to re-establish part of the Delaware Canal filled in for parking at the Levittown Shopping Center.

unhurried and charming Bucks County summer home was steeped in the spirit of humanitarianism. This reconstructed, 43-acre plantation features a manor house with period furnishings, outbuildings, livestock and gardens, all of which serve as a fine example of country life for the well-off and elite of the day (400 Pennsbury Memorial Road, Morrisville, PA 19067; 215-946-0400; www.pennsburymanor.org).

Levittown

In 1951 an exhibit center displaying samples of three houses opened along Route 13 in Tullytown. One model, the Levittowner, cost $9,990 and required

Bristol

Victorian mansions, a vital riverfront, and a touch of nature at trail's end

Construction of the Delaware Canal was a major development for Bristol's economy.

The southern terminus of the D&L Trail was first settled by Europeans in 1681. Bristol's prime location helped make it a busy port and industrial town in the 1800s. Coal yards and warehouses sprang up along the canal, as did large mills that manufactured carpets, woolens and other textiles. Later, shipyards thrived and the neighborhoods still show signs of modest worker housing, along with elegant Victorian homes. The last portion of the Delaware Canal flowed through town, through a lagoon and into the basin near Bristol Marsh.

Bristol is the oldest town in Bucks County and the third oldest in Pennsylvania. Its Delaware Riverfront resembles a New England seaport because 1917 brought the Merchant Shipbuilding Corporation. Shipbuilders and other yard workers poured into the town vicinity. During World War II, the shipyards were converted for use in the manufacturing of aircraft. After the war, people stayed in Bristol and the population continued to rise. By the 1960s though, the factories stood abandoned and the following years brought slower development. The growth that did occur was largely due to the generosity of Joseph Ridgway Grundy, industrialist and politician. Through his last will and testament, he created The Grundy

The clocktower at the Grundy Mill complex was a landmark for canalers.

Foundation, a philanthropic organization dedicated to improving Bristol and other communities in Bucks County.

Today, Bristol hosts special events at river's edge, providing a perfect opportunity to stroll, shop or dine within the 50-site Radcliffe Street Historic District. Along the restored riverfront you'll find Victorian mansions, including the Margaret R. Grundy Museum. The house was built in 1818 but the Grundy family, wealthy owners of local textile

mills, didn't buy it until 1884. The interior offers a look at the style of elegant, luxurious living some people enjoyed at the turn of the century. Woodwork imported from Europe is found throughout the house, including carved oak paneling and staircase in the entrance foyer. The living room, accented with cherry wood, features a fireplace with a unique double flue that frames a stained glass window. The large, paneled dining room, with its unique and unusual angles and arches, contains an Italian carpet designed

Bristol, Pa.
1681

to fit the room, a magnificently carved oak table, and a variety of other extravagant furnishings.

The Grundy Museum is located in the heart of Bristol and the sizeable property runs along the Delaware River. The former residence of Joseph R. Grundy is dedicated to the memory of his sister, Margaret. Two floors are open to the public and admission is free (open weekdays 1 p.m. to 4 p.m., Saturdays

Silver Lake was formed in the early 1700s when Otter Creek was dammed to power a mill on Mill Street. Throughout the years the lake (once known as Mill Lake) has become a recreation area, and in 1972 the Bucks County Department of Parks and Recreation created the Silver Lake Nature Center. Today this 235-acre sanctuary offers a variety of activities for individuals, families and groups. There are three miles of trails that carry you through a variety of habi-

Local initiative made the restoration of the lagoon at Bristol possible.

1 p.m. to 3 p.m.). The Margaret R. Grundy Library can also be explored. Bristol Borough also the site of the landmark Grundy Mill with its easy-to-spot clock tower.

Elsewhere in Bristol, a National Park Service plan in the 1980s resulted in a walking trail along an old railroad spur line right-of-way.

Nearby you'll find the Silver Lake Nature Center (1306 Bath Rd.; 215-785-1177).

tat that's home to more than 160 species of birds, raccoons, muskrats, opossum, deer, and other mammals and reptiles. This part of the state is known geographically as the Coastal Plain. Its geology, vegetation and wildlife are unique.

For additional information:
Bristol Borough Business Association
131 Mill Street
Bristol, PA 19007
215-788-4288
www.bristolborough.com

Credits and Contributors

Photo Credits:

Kristi Cochios
Elissa G. Marsden
Sherry Acevedo
George Harvan
Bill & Lorraine Mineo
Bonnie Tobin, Delaware Canal State Park
Bucks County Conference & Visitors Bureau
Diane Madl, Hickory Run State Park Complex
Everett Kaul, Walnutport Canal Association
John Sikora Photography
Karen Williamson, Heritage Conservancy
Lehigh Valley Convention & Visitors Bureau
Marianne Dubresson, Bucks County Parks & Recreation
National Canal Museum, Easton, PA
Pennsylvania Fish & Boat Commission
Pennsylvania Game Commission
Susan Taylor, Friends of the Delaware Canal
Tom Gettings, Wildlands Conservancy
Wyoming Valley Levee Project
Simone Jaffe Collins Landscape Architecture
Hub Willson Photography

Contributors:

Allen Sachse, Bill Mineo, Sherry Acevedo, Rayne Schnabel, Dale Freudenberger, Denise Holub (D&L Staff), Doug Reynolds (Staff Consultant), Camille Lore (Intern); Lance Metz, Charlie Derr and Tom Smith (National Canal Museum); Susan Taylor (Friends of the Delaware Canal); Sean Sullivan (Heritage Conservancy); Bonnie Tobin (DCNR); Annie Sanders and Charles Petrillo (D&L Commissioners).